Collins gem

Fossils

Douglas Palmer

HarperCollins Publishers Ltd.
77–85 Fulham Palace Road
London
W6 8JB

www.collins.co.uk

First published in 2006

10 09 08 07 06
10 9 8 7 6 5 4 3 2 1

A catalogue record for this book is available from the British Library.

ISBN-10: 0 00 722254 8
ISBN-13: 978 0 00 722254 4

Picture credits:
pp70, 96, 105, 109, 110, 117, 118, 128, 135, 144, 146 © www.fossilmuseum.net; pp16, 41, 44, 45, 49, 50, 52, 55, 61, 66, 67, 71, 77, 78, 88, 89, 92, 94, 131, 137 © Geoscience Features; pp42, 46, 58, 68, 81, 84, 90, 102, 107, 108, 116, 126, 127, 130, 150, 157, 168, 171 © The Natural History Museum, London; p121 © Michael Long/NHMPL; pp124-125, 165 © John Sibbick/NHMPL; p139 © Geological Museum of China/NHMPL; p174 © Sumio Harada/FLPA

The author and publishers would like to thank Ross Secord at the Museum of Paleontology, The University of Michigan for his help in reading and advising on the manuscript for this book.

Edited and designed by D & N Publishing, Lambourn Woodlands, Berkshire
Printed and bound in Italy by Amadeus

CONTENTS

INTRODUCTION

Around 49 million years ago, in Early Eocene times, Messel in Germany was a wooded lakeland inhabited by a wonderful diversity of life. A time-traveller would recognize many of the plants and creatures living there, including the snakes, bats, birds and insects. However, other creatures would seem out of place in Europe today. Altogether there were 35 different kinds of mammals including anteaters, pangolins, large hedgehog-like creatures, opossums and lemur-like primates. There was also a small-dog-sized mammal with hooves on its toes, known as *Propalaeotherium*, which was one of the earliest horses.

Many of the plants would also be familiar, the laurel, oaks and occasional conifers, but alongside them grew more exotic kinds for northern Europe – palms and citrus trees. Most noticeable to us would be the absence of grasses, which had yet to develop.

We can reconstruct the original scene at Messel in such detail because the lakebed sediments preserved their fossils in wonderful detail, which includes soft tissues such as hair on the mammals and feathers on the birds. Scientists have been able to study the plant and animal fossils because so many have been carefully collected and preserved over decades of collecting from the site. Such is the wealth of fossil material at Messel that it has been declared a World Heritage Site.

Modern analysis of the biota reveals creatures that were thought to be restricted to South America and Asia today. This part of Europe enjoyed a warm temperate climate at the time and was clearly something of a crossroads for migratory animals, many of which subsequently died out as the climate became cooler.

Lakeside life at Messel some 49 million years ago

Unfortunately, rock strata with such well-preserved fossils are rare. As we shall see, most of the fossil record is made up of fossils that do not preserve as much information about the original organisms or the environments in which they lived. Even so, scientists who study fossils (palaeontologists) can recover a surprising amount of information by working like detectives, searching for clues from fossilized shells, bones and teeth. The way they are preserved and the surrounding sediments and their chemistry tell us about where they lived and where they were buried.

WHAT ARE FOSSILS?

Fossils are the remains of once living organisms preserved in ancient sediments and rock strata. As such they are the main evidence for past life and its complex evolutionary history of originations and extinctions. Fossil 'remains' vary enormously, from organic molecules that may be billions of years old to footprints of our extinct human relatives and entire skeletons of animals ranging from fish to dinosaurs. Very rarely are delicate organic structures such as DNA, muscle fibres, feathers, hair or flowers fossilized.

Most fossils are made of the toughest and least destructible parts of past organisms. For instance, common plant fossils include microscopic pollen grains and, at the other end of the scale, large pieces of woody tissue found in coal deposits.

The most abundant fossils are seashells. They range from the microscopic shells of unicellular organisms such as foraminifers (*see* p.80) to those of the more familiar clams that still inhabit our seashores. The bones and teeth of vertebrates are generally much less common.

Altogether, the proportion of life that has any chance of being fossilized is very small. The actual fossil record is highly biased towards common organisms with relatively indestructible hard parts such as shells, bones, teeth or woody tissues. This bias is emphasized by the nature of the sedimentary rock record, which tends to preserve large volumes of shallow sea sediments. Nevertheless, some important geological environments do preserve large volumes of land-based sediment and land-dwelling organisms.

Recognition of fossils as the remains of past life was achieved by some ancient scholars such as Xenophanes of Colphon (*c.* 570–490 BC). However, many other scholars were puzzled by the strange mixture of organic form and inorganic composition presented by some fossils. And, there were additonal problems. How to interpret the presence of seashell-like fossils on inland mountain tops, and why so many fossils were not the same as living creatures – had some become extinct?

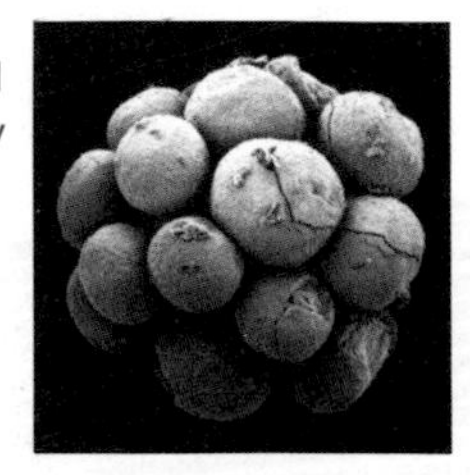

A minute cluster of embryonic cells from China, 570 million years old

We have to remember that the early development of the study of fossils, known as palaeontology (meaning the study of ancient life), took place in a very different cultural environment. It was only when the scientific evidence for the nature of fossils and their distribution in time and space became so overwhelming that the old interpretations gave way, but that did not happen until the early decades of the 19th century.

HOW ARE FOSSILS PRESERVED?

Under certain rare conditions, such as within ice and amber, the remains of ancient organisms can be preserved almost in their entirety. Even ancient DNA may be preserved in frozen bodies tens of thousands of years old, such as within the famous Siberian mammoths.

The remains of an insect or frog preserved in fossilized tree resin, known as amber, may be perfectly preserved externally but their DNA has not survived (*see* p.26). Amber-embedded organisms are

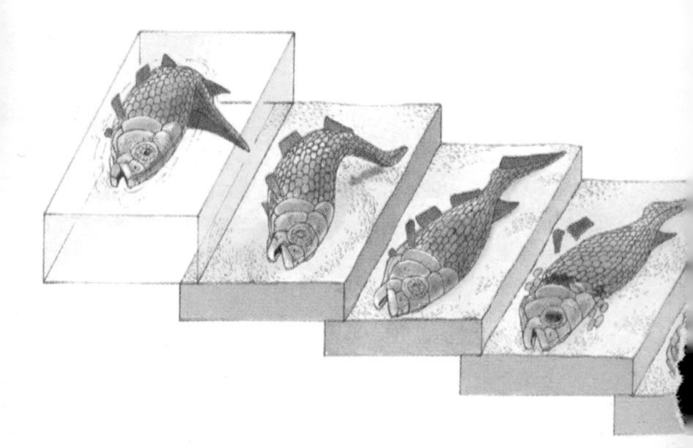

This fish is still fairly intact before burial and fossilization

known from Upper Triassic rock strata some 225 million years old. But these are unusual circumstances for fossil preservation; by far the majority of fossils are preserved by more complex processes in which the original residual material is altered in some way.

To understand how fossils are preserved it is necessary to know something about what happens to organisms after they die and the processes by which their remains are recruited to the rock and fossil record. Upon death most organic remains are scavenged by other organisms, ranging in size from big cats down to insect larvae and microbes. The economy of nature is such that most organic matter is recycled unless the organism died in circumstances that prevented scavenging and decay. Very cold and dry or oxygen-poor conditions are ideal for slowing down the processes of decay and degradation.

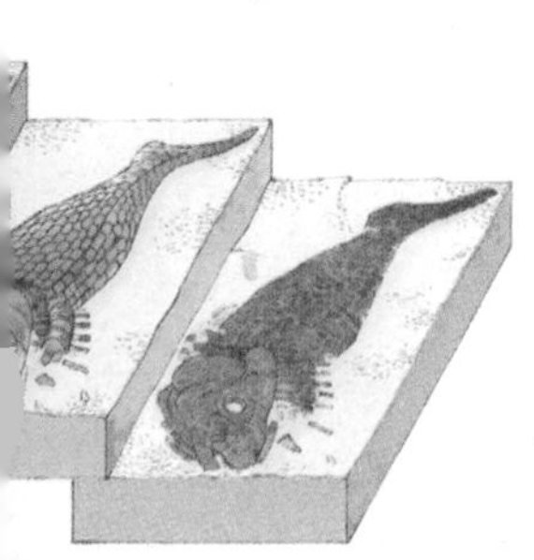

Generally, soft tissues are removed by scavengers within days or weeks of death, leaving only the toughest and most indestructible hard parts such as shells, bones and teeth. Most of these skeletal materials are composed of inorganic minerals plus a small amount of organic matter. However, in plants and some animals the residual material is wholly or largely organic, composed of compounds such as protein, lignin or waxes. Prolonged exposure at Earth's surface will gradually destroy even these potential fossil remains through a combination of chemical and physical processes. For fossilization to occur, the remains have to be buried or enclosed in a material that will protect them from further destruction.

For instance, the remains of sea life that typically accumulates on beaches is composed mostly of

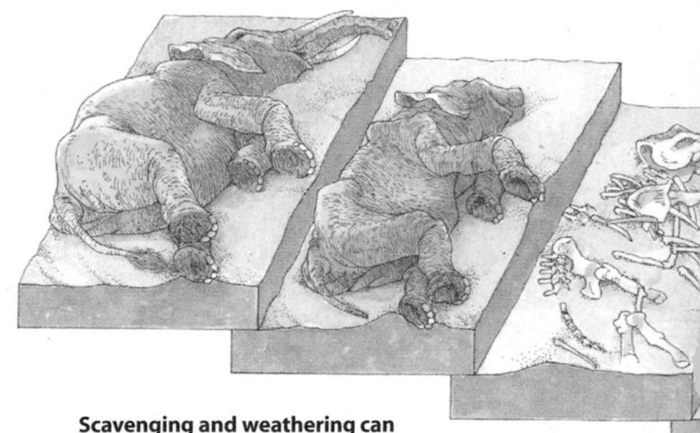

Scavenging and weathering can lead to information loss before burial and fossilization

seashells derived from common clams and snails. There may also be bits of crabs, sea urchins, algae and even occasional remains of fish, seabirds or land-derived plants lying on the shore below high water. But If you dig into the shore deposits, most of the remains are those of shells. If there are pebbles on the beach, they will soon destroy any shells caught in the surf.

Even when buried beneath layers of sediment, further geological processes of deeper burial have to take place in order to prevent reworking and destruction of the remains by normal processes of erosion on land and beneath the sea.

Once enclosed in sediment and buried beneath an increasing load of younger sediments, organic remains are subject to further change. Ground water is rarely neutral in its chemistry and, if slightly acidic, may dissolve shells and bone completely. The enclosing sediment sometimes moulds the shape of the shell and, when hardened into rock, may preserve that shape. Enough detail can remain on the sediment mould for experts to identify the species.

The internal space, originally filled by the shell or bone, may be refilled with sediment or mineral to form a cast, which again can sometimes be identified. Replacement and mineralization commonly occur, especially where the original fossil material is unstable. For instance, the carbonate mineral aragonite is common in mollusc shells and is usually replaced by the more stable calcite or dolomite. Mineralization by completely different minerals can also occur, for example, the introduction of silica to porous wood or bone may occasionally mineralize their tissues through the addition of or replacement by siliceous opal or agate.

As sediment is compressed and changed into rock, the original shape of fossil remains is often distorted, mostly by flattening, but also sometimes by other tectonic deformation as part of mountain building. In extreme conditions the fossils may become unrecognizable, but there are techniques for imaging deformed fossils and correcting the deformation. The extent of deformation is itself useful for informing us about the extent to which the surrounding geological environment has been deformed by earth processes.

It was these often complex processes of mineralization and deformation that confused past scholars when they were trying to work out whether fossils had grown within rock strata or represented the altered remains of once-living organisms.

EXCEPTIONAL PRESERVATION

From the investigations of fossils during the first decades of the 19th century, it was realized that some rock strata preserved fossils much better than others. Mining and quarrying of particular rock types uncovered famous fossils, such as the earliest bird *Archaeopteryx*. Indeed, from the late 18th century onwards the fine-grained limestones around Solnhofen and Eichstatt in Bavaria, southern Germany, were renowned throughout Europe for their beautifully preserved fossils.

These slabs of limestone strata of Jurassic age were used for lithographic printing, but were also found to contain a huge variety of different fossils, from dragonflies to fish. And, most famously in 1861, the remains of a small feathered bird were found. Called *Archaeopteryx*, it was seen as one of the best fossll examples of Darwin's theory of evolution by natural selection (*see* p.25).

Palaeontologists now realize that certain sedimentary environments and geological processes can promote exceptional preservation of organic remains. As we have seen, the process of fossilization normally removes all but the most durable remains of organisms, so there is very little record of soft-bodied creatures. But by targeting the right kinds of rocks throughout the geological record, it has become

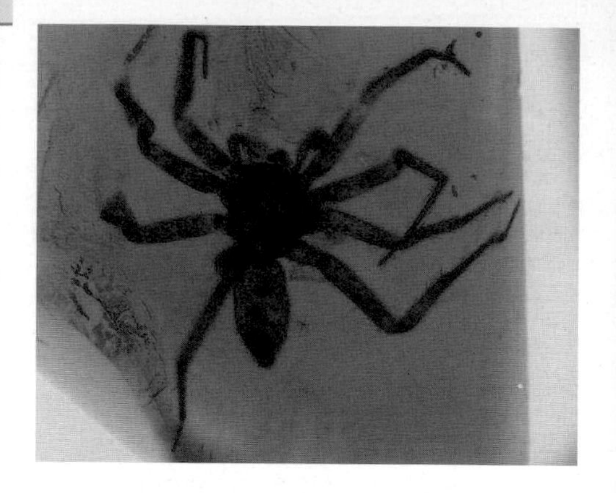

Spiders are common arthropods but they are rarely fossilized; this one is 'embalmed' in amber

possible to open privileged windows on the life of the past that is not normally preserved. These give a much better idea of the total diversity of past life in these environments.

For instance, the most common animals alive today are insects, with nearly a million known species (compared with around 5,000 mammal species). The total known rock record contains around 500,000 fossil species for the whole history of life and, of these, the known fossil insect species only amount to a few thousand. Insect bodies tend to be relatively delicate and their remains are readily destroyed by sedimentary processes, except in certain exceptional low energy environments such as lakes and lagoons. Here their remains may become embedded and preserved in fine-grained muddy sediments where there is little or no biological activity such as burrowing.

A good example is the Eocene lake deposits of Florissant, Colorado. About 34 million years old, they preserve remarkable details of a wonderful diversity of insects, fish, plants and birds. Even mosses, fruits and flowers and colour markings on butterfly wings can be seen in the now monochrome fossils. And this is despite being flattened between layers of very fine volcanic ash, which rained down onto the lake waters from a nearby volcano.

Unusual mineralization or entrapment in a good preservative medium, such as amber, oil tar or peat, can also conserve tissues and organisms not normally found in the fossil record. Amber is perhaps the most famous of such preserving media. Within it a whole host of organisms from bacteria to frogs and lizards has been preserved with exceptional detail. Unfortunately, the hope that fossil DNA might also be preserved within amber insects has not been supported by rigorous analysis.

However, our knowledge of fossil insects has been enhanced enormously by the amber record. Sadly, there were relatively few geological situations where resin-producing trees flourished and their amber recruited to the sediment record. Tiny amber-like rodlets of resin have been recovered from Carboniferous deposits but so far they are unfossiliferous. Triassic-age amber, some 225 million years old, has been found to contain well-preserved single-celled amoebae. The oldest amber insects come from Cretaceous amber in Lebanon (around 125 million years old), but most famous of all are the Palaeogene amber deposits of the Baltic (around 38 million years old) and the Dominican Republic (between 20 and 40 million years old).

Rapid mineralization of body tissues can produce spectacular fossils, but generally on a small scale. Through the activities of bacteria associated with the degradation of tissue, certain phosphorous and iron minerals can be precipitated over soft tissue. These durable minerals not only replicate tissue surfaces at a very fine scale but may subsequently survive for hundreds of millions of years. Amongst the most famous of recent finds of this kind are the late Precambrian Doushantuo embryos from rocks in China that are about 570 million years old. These microscopic fossils are the fertilized embryos of various invertebrates, such as sponges, that have been preserved by a phosphate mineral and show all stages of early development from first cleavage onwards.

THE VARIETY OF LIFE AND ITS CLASSIFICATION

Living organisms have a huge range of diversity, size and complexity from microscopic viruses to the 2,000-tonne giant redwood trees that grow to 100m high and 150-tonne blue whales that grow to over 30m in length. Over its 3.8 billion year history, life has evolved from microscopic to bigger, more complex and more diverse organisms. By the Late Devonian, around 370 million years ago, life had not only colonized the land but diversified to include tree-sized plants and vertebrates (commonly known as backboned animals). By the Late Jurassic, around 150 million years ago, all the major groups of vertebrates from fish to mammals were established. Some of the dinosaurs would dwarf today's largest land-living animals – the elephants. Giant plant-eating sauropods grew to over 40m long and over 80 tonnes in weight.

Current estimates put the total number of described living species at around 1.5 million, of which nearly 1 million are insects. The total diversity of life today may be anywhere between 7 and 20 million species. But so far only some 500,000 species of fossils have been described from our record of life's long evolution and diversification.

To the layperson it might seem a bit odd that scientists do not even know how many different kinds of organisms have been named and described, let alone how many kinds of organisms there are alive today. By comparison, the fact that we do not know how many fossil organisms have lived and died throughout the history of life on Earth might seem a bit more excusable.

To understand the problem, we have to remember that less than 250 years ago, in 1758 when the Swedish botanist Carl Linnaeus first published the 10th edition of his classification of living organisms, the list totalled less than 12,000 species of plants and animals. Since then scientists all over the world have tried to describe, illustrate and name the wonderful variety of life on Earth. Their results have been published in many different languages and hundreds of thousands of publications, many of which were not widely distributed. As a result it has been very difficult to synthesize such a volume of information of varying quality, but computerization of data and worldwide cooperation via the Internet promises to make the task more feasible.

Classification of all this life is traditionally founded upon what is called the Latin binomial ('two-name' – genus and species) system formalized by Linnaeus. Thus populations of organisms that can interbreed to produce viable young are called species and are put within a genus grouping that may contain one or more closely related species. For instance, the genus

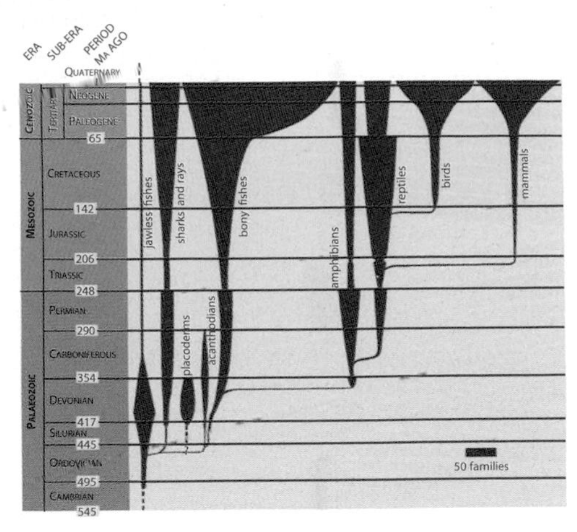

The pattern of vertebrate evolution has changed significantly over time

Homo contains at least six species, all of which are extinct except our species *Homo sapiens*. Biological species have a genetic basis and are different from most extinct fossil species, which are established on physical characters derived from their preserved remains. The essential breeding test cannot be applied to fossil species. They are essentially the constructs of scientists as are other higher level taxonomic

Different plant groups have dominated land vegetation at different times

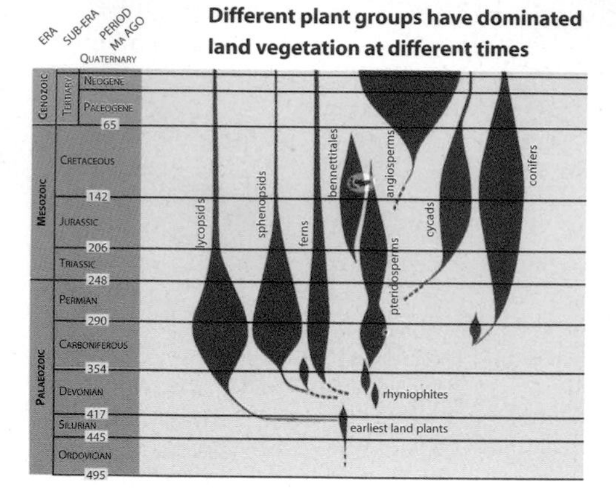

Linnean (a) and cladistic (b) classifications emphasize different aspects of biological relationships

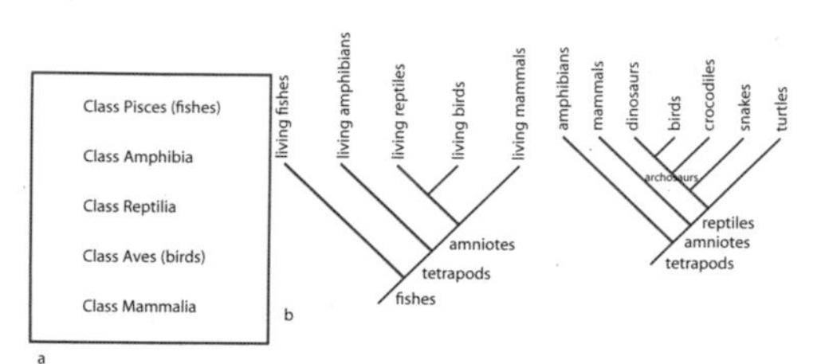

groupings from the genus upwards through families, orders, classes, phyla and so on. However, some of these groupings do almost certainly reflect genuinely close biological relationships.

In recent years a new method of classification called cladistics has been developed and widely accepted as an extension to the traditional Linnaean system. Its aim is to establish a branching (clade means branch) family tree or hierarchy of ancestral relations. Ideally this hierarchy extends back to the beginning and thus encompasses all life. These relationships are established on the basis of shared derived characters, with descendent sister taxa grouped according to their most recent common ancestor. The problem with the method and its application to fossils is that it can be difficult to identify which characters are derived. The result is that often there are a number of different possible branching schemes. Also, cladistic analysis lends itself to statistical analysis and produces many more branching points than traditional Linnaean classification.

Linnaeus originally recognized just two kingdoms of living organisms: plants and animals. By the 1960s, understanding of the microscopic organisms and their cellular structure showed that five kingdoms can be recognized: bacteria (Monera), Protista (protozoans), fungi, plants and animals. Furthermore, they can be grouped into two major categories: the single-celled prokaryotes, without a true nuclear membrane, and the eukaryotes, which have a nucleus in each cell enclosed by a true nuclear membrane. The latter are generally larger and more complex and include all the multicellular organisms plus many unicells. Analysis of the genetic structure of sample organisms from within the original five kingdoms showed the microbial world to be far more complex than previously thought. Now the prokaryotes are divided into two domains, Bacteria and Archaea, with the Eukarya forming a third separate domain. The Eukarya include a huge range of organisms from the amoebas to red algae, green algae, green land plants, fungi and animals.

For the most part the fossil record can only inform us about a small portion of these three domains, namely the green land plants and animals plus occasional windows into the microscopic world of the prokaryotes and protistan eukaryotes.

EVOLUTION AND EXTINCTION

Since time immemorial, animals and plants have been grouped like with like. Major groupings, such as fish, amphibians, birds, reptiles and mammals, have been recognized by many different cultures. Each culture also had its creation myth, which invoked a deity or deities and tended to place humankind in some sort of special or favoured category.

By the 19th century there were a number of more scientifically based theories about the evolution of life, but by the latter part of the century the Darwin–Wallace theory of evolution by natural selection and adaptation came to dominate scientific explanation for the history and diversity of life. It was supported by growing understanding of the facts of reproduction and inheritance. Further evidence came from the fossil record of evolving lineages, such as in the horse family, and rare transitional forms were found, which preserved characteristics derived from their ancestral group. For example, the early bird *Archaeopteryx* preserves a long, bony reptilian tail and toothed beak-like jaw (*see* pp.136–8).

Widespread scientific acceptance of evolution by natural selection has resulted from the discovery of the mechanisms of inheritance, the genetic code, the double helix structure of DNA and its replication. The genetic code (genome) of several different organisms, from the humble yeast to that of humans, has been outlined now. We can describe and analyse the genetic basis for species and the evolution of populations with common gene pools. We can understand how speciation happens through separation of gene pools over time and the development of distinct characteristics through mutation.

Unfortunately, DNA is a fragile protein and degrades quickly after death. Ancient DNA can be preserved only in exceptional circumstances and even then it is fragmentary. The recovery of fossil DNA is so far restricted to tissues that are a few tens of thousands of years old. However, DNA from bones of Neanderthals has verified that they were a distinct species, and not the direct ancestors of modern Europeans as was thought at one time.

Given the long history of life, it is inevitable that 99.99 per cent of the different kinds of organisms that have ever lived are extinct. Nevertheless, we humans still carry encoded genetic material that can be found in some of the simplest organisms. Evolution is the only mechanism known that can have allowed such a transfer of genetic information through so many different kinds of organisms over billions of years. During this lengthy history of adaptation and development species have constantly died off, and some major extinction events have wiped out whole groups of organisms.

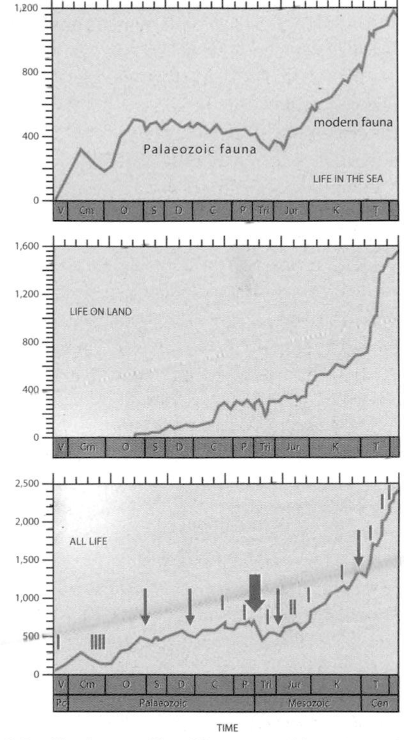

Fossil families have suffered 'booms' and 'busts' over time

Five major episodes of extinction over the last 450 million years have now been recognized. The largest of these occurred at the end of the Permian (about 251 million years ago) and had a major impact upon life. It has been estimated that 90 per cent of marine and 70 per cent of land-living species were wiped out. The exact cause is still not known, but there are a number of possible contributing factors, such as volcanism producing climate change and possible changes in the chemistry of the oceans. The more famous but less catastrophic extinction at the end of the Cretaceous (about 65 million years ago) 'only' wiped out some 60 per cent of species. The event is better known because it included the dinosaurs and is associated with a very dramatic event – the collision of a large extra-terrestrial body (some 11km in diameter) with Earth.

Darwin went to great lengths to explain why he did not use fossil evidence to support his theory of evolution. He was well aware of how incomplete the fossil record is and knew that many palaeontologists did not support his theory. Today, Darwin would not have been able to avoid the fossil record because it provides a wealth of evidence for the evolution of life on Earth over the last 3.8 billion years. This can be seen at all levels from species-by-species change within hundreds of thousands of years to large-scale expansion and decline of whole groups of organisms, such as the dinosaurs.

THE DISTRIBUTION OF FOSSILS THROUGH TIME

The earliest fossils are chemical traces of life that perhaps date back some 3.8 billion years. Traces of microbial life, known as stromatolites, are recorded in the rock record from 3.5 billion years ago. But it took life a long time before multicelled organisms managed to grow to any significant size and reproduce sexually. Not until some 600 million years ago does the fossil record preserve remains that can be readily recognized with the unaided eye. But from about 540 million years ago life has, at times, diversified at an astonishing rate – a phenomenon that is quite well recorded by fossil remains but is by no means complete.

The vast majority of the known fossil record has been recovered from the shells, bones, teeth and carbon traces of animals and plants that have lived throughout the last 542 million years of Earth history. This is known as the Phanerozoic Eon, which lasted from the Cambrian to the present. However, the vast majority of geological time and early history of Earth and life is hidden away in the 4-billion-year-long record of late Precambrian rocks. Until the late 19th century it was generally thought that this whole protracted phase of Earth history was devoid of fossil remains.

Evolutionists were aware that life had to originate within Precambrian times because the earliest

Cambrian rocks preserve a range of animals from sponges to trilobites that must have a more ancient ancestry. The assumption was that Precambrian life was microscopic and soft bodied and therefore not preserved as fossils.

Thanks to several decades of intrepid sleuthing by generations of palaeontologists and numerous lucky finds, we now have a fossil record that extends back some 3.8 billion years. These earliest fossils are just chemical traces of complex organic molecules, but their synthesis required the presence of living organisms. A more tangible and visible record appears around 3.5 billion years ago in the form of fossil-related structures known as stromatolites. These are layered mounds of sediment up to a metre or so high and wide, that formed in shallow tropical waters and were probably built up by microbial mats that trapped sediment. Similar structures with microbial mats still exist today in the Gulf of Mexico and Western Australia.

It is important to realize that the evolution of life happened within radically changing environments. Ocean and atmospheric chemistry was evolving and the configuration of the oceans and continents was constantly being rearranged by ocean-floor spreading and the movement of tectonic plates.

The prokaryotic bacterial microbes that build stromatolites use energy from the Sun to fuel photosynthesis, and as a by-product release oxygen into the atmosphere. Numerous spores, organic cyst-like structures and occasional bacterial filaments are now known as a fossil record of this long slow phase of life's early evolution. Famous localities include the 3.46-billion-year-old Apex Chert of Western Australia, and Gunflint Chert of western Ontario, Canada (about 2 billion years old). It was the activity of such organisms that gradually increased atmospheric oxygen levels and allowed the evolution of eukaryotic micro-organisms that depended upon this gas for 'breathing' (respiration). About 2 billion years passed before life evolved multicellular organisms, but they were still confined to the oceans of the world.

A succession of major glacial episodes (so-called 'snowball' Earth events) may have alternately caused extinctions and originations within early life, but scientists are still trying to gain a better understanding of the biological impact of these events. We do know that by 600 million years ago marine life had diversified and produced a range of soft-bodied organisms that grew several centimetres in size and exceptionally up to 2m long. These are known as the Ediacaran fauna, named after a locality in South Australia where well-preserved fossils were first found.

The exact biological nature of the ediacarans has puzzled experts. They consist of various discs, fronds and sac-like forms that lived both on and within the seabed. Some show distinct similarities to existing organisms such as the seapens (pennatulaceans). Their fossils are now known from most continents and many had worldwide distributions, but most had died out by the beginning of the Cambrian period, 542 million years ago.

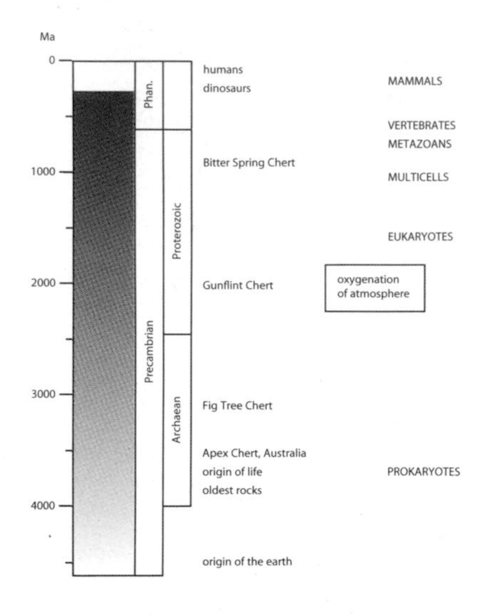

Life was very slow to evolve from water-dwelling microbes and most fossil remains are less than 545 million years old

There was a remarkable explosion of different life forms at the beginning of the Cambrian, marked by the appearance of many small shelly fossils. There seems to have been a marine arms race and a proliferation of predators that resulted in survival of those that were armoured with shells or skeletons, or possessed escape mechanisms such as swimming or burrowing. By Middle Cambrian times most of the marine invertebrate groups had evolved, as had the chordates – animals with the beginnings of vertebrate characters – and the earliest vertebrates themselves.

By the Late Ordovician, around 450 million years ago, primitive moss-like bryophyte plants and millipede-like arthropods had invaded the land for the first time and armoured jawless fish-like animals were becoming increasingly common in the seas. By the end of the Ordovician period, around 440 million years ago, there was a major glacial episode that is well recorded in the rocks of North Africa, which lay near the South Pole at the time.

The colonization of the land and fresh waters by primitive plants and animals continued through Silurian times, although most plants were small and confined to water-logged riverside and seaside environments. The evolution of jawed fish produced a whole new level of size increase and competition in the seas. Until this time, few creatures were bigger than a metre in size.

The amalgamation of North America and northern Europe to form a tropical supercontinent by the Late Devonian around 370 million years ago, coincided with the evolution of the first tree-sized plants and the first four-limbed vertebrates. The latter were still initially water dwelling, but soon used their limbs to move out of the water.

By the Carboniferous period forests had become widespread throughout lowland tropics and their accumulated remains formed the first extensive coal deposits. The first reptiles with shelled eggs became independent of water whilst some early amphibians grew to crocodile size. By the Permian period, deserts had become widespread throughout the tropics of the Gondwanaland supercontinent, but in polar regions there was a widespread glaciation from the Late Carboniferous through Permian times. The end of the Permian period and the Palaeozoic era was marked by the most catastrophic extinction event in the history of life, probably as a result of climate change in combination with other possible factors such as large-scale lava eruption and changes in the chemistry of the oceans and atmosphere.

The three successive periods of the Mesozoic era – the Triassic, Jurassic and Cretaceous – are famous for the rise and fall of the reptiles both on land, at sea and in the air. But they also saw the early evolution of the birds, flowering plants and placental mammals. The Gondwanan supercontinent broke up with the opening of the Atlantic and Tethys oceans, with widespread flooding of low-lying continental margins. The end of the Cretaceous period and the end of the era is marked by another major extinction event, which coincides with a catastrophic impact event 65 million years ago. Many reptile groups became extinct, along with the ammonites and other invertebrates.

The Cenozoic era has seen the rise of the mammals on land, in the sea and in the air, replacing many of the dominant reptiles. But the reptiles also recovered and evolved many new crocodiles, lizards, snakes, turtles and tortoises. On land the flowering plants became increasingly successful and diverse, from grasses to large trees, many of which are pollinated by animals, especially insects. The latter part of the era has seen global cooling and then successive glaciations with intervening warmer phases from around 2 million years ago. Primates evolved throughout the era with some 20 human-related species evolving and dying out over the last 6 million years to leave just one species, *Homo sapiens*, alive today.

THE FOSSIL RECORD: ANIMALS WITHOUT BACKBONES

PRECAMBRIAN FOSSILS

Precambrian fossils are now known from strata around 3.7–3.8 billion years old and show that life must have originated early in the history of Earth. For over 3 billion years this life was probably entirely microbial and confined to the oceans and seas. That life should have such a long slow 'fuse' is something of a puzzle, but it took a long time for the chemistry of the early oceans and atmosphere to become sufficiently oxygenated for the evolution of complex multicellular organisms dependent upon oxygen for respiration.

The earliest fossils

There have been several claims that particles of graphite (a carbon mineral) found in early Precambrian sedimentary strata deposited around 3.7–3.8 billion years ago (bya) in southwest Greenland have an organic origin. Further claims that their carbon isotopes even indicate an origin from photosynthesizing organisms have now been discounted and there is still much argument about the true origin of these minerals.

Stromatolites

The oldest generally accepted fossils are a kind of trace fossil consisting of laminated mounds of sediment some 3.5 billion years old from Australia (Apex Chert). Living stromatolites from warm tropical shallow-waters (for example Hamelin Pool, Western Australia) show that they are generated by microbial mats of cyanobacteria and algae that grow up from the seabed and trap thin layers of sediment, forming distinctive mounds up to 1m high. Stromatolites can be identified from 3.5 billion years ago to the present, however, they were relatively common from 3.2–0.54 billion years ago.

Stromatolitic mounds of sediment from Greenland made by Precambrian microbes about 2.5 million years ago

Organic filaments and cysts

The oldest actual body fossils are 2 billion-year-old organic cellular filaments and unicells preserved in the Gunflint Cherts of western Ontario, Canada and the Duck Creek Dolomite of Western Australia. They resemble the prokaryote cyanobacteria that still form stromatolite mounds today. Throughout the Precambrian, microbes of this kind diversified in the world's oceans and seas and their fossil record is becoming much better known.

Eroded stromatolites from the Gunflint Chert beside Lake Superior, Canada, found by Stanley Tyler in 1953

Ediacaran fauna

Fossils were first found in upper Precambrian sandstone strata of the Ediacaran Hills of South Australia by Australian geologist Reginald Sprigg in 1946. Now some 100 ediacaran species are known from strata of this age (565–543 million years ago), and possibly younger (480 million years ago), around the world.

Ranging from 1cm to 2m in size, they have a variety of shapes from hemispherical blobs (for example, *Beltanelliformis*) to flat ribbed discs (for example, *Dickinsonia*) and ribbons to feather-shaped fronds (for example, *Charnia*) and sac-like bodies (*Pteridinium*), and all are entirely soft-bodied and preserved as sediment moulds.

Initially the ediacaran fossils were all shoehorned into existing invertebrate groups such as jellyfish and even trilobites, but now it is acknowledged that only a few, such as the seapen-like (pennatulacean) *Charnia*, can be so placed. Expert opinion is divided about their affinities – some think that they are extinct coelenterates (like soft corals and jellyfish) whilst others think that they might even be an unknown group of giant unicells.

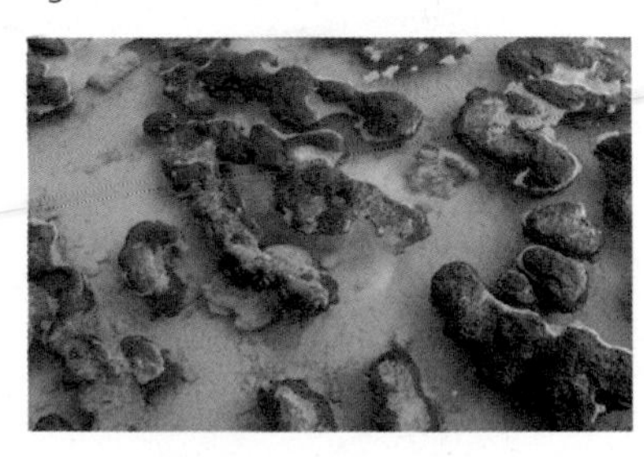

Modern stromatolites from Western Australia

SPONGES, ARCHAEOCYATHANS, CORALS, BRYOZOANS

Luckily for palaeontologists, many biologically simple organisms such as sponges, archaeocyathans, corals and bryozoans secrete mineralized skeletons and have considerable potential to become preserved as fossils, mostly in the rock record of seabed deposits. As a result we can trace the evolution, extinction and important ecological development through time of these animals that live by filtering tiny food particles from the water. Biologically they are interesting, as many reproduce by asexual budding to produce large colonies as well as reproducing successive generations sexually.

Different combinations of these organisms have built reefs ranging in scale from small archaeocyathid mud mounds to the biggest organic related structures on Earth such as the modern Australian Great Barrier Reef. Reefs play an important role in the sedimentary rock record and economic geology as sites for hydrocarbons and mineral ore bodies.

Sponges

Biologically, sponges are remarkable animals and are placed in the phylum Porifera. Sponges form a colony of single cells that cooperate together as a multicellular organism. Individual colonies grow from the seabed or other hard surface to around 1m in size.

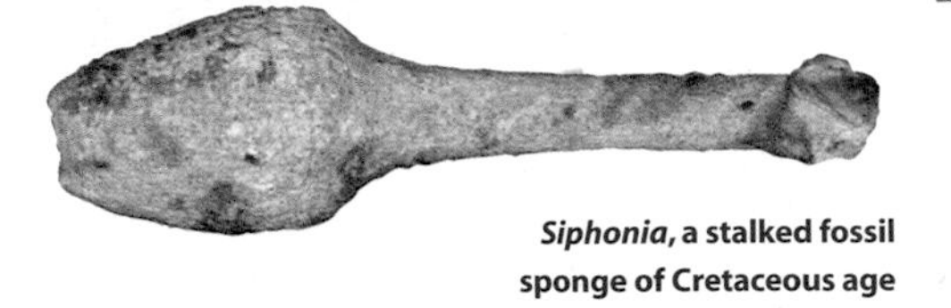

***Siphonia*, a stalked fossil sponge of Cretaceous age**

Sponges have highly porous walls supported by various skeletal materials such as spicules of silica (glass sponges), calcium carbonate (calcareous sponges) or protein (bath sponges) or combinations of these. Their classification into three classes is based partly on the composition of their skeletons: the Hexactinellida (glass sponges with silica spicules), the Calcarea (calcisponges with calcareous skeletons) and the Demospongiae (with skeletons of mixed composition).

Sponges are very variable in form but most have a basic vase shape. The main opening of the body carries water out of the body, having entered through the walls driven by special flagellated cells.

Their fossil record ranges from Late Precambrian to the present and at times they have been so abundant as to form reefs, such as the Capitan Reef of Permian age In Texas, which extends for some 500km.

Today there are 10,000 or so species of sponges living in both marine and fresh waters and at all water depths, with some particularly beautiful glass sponges living in ocean depths of up to 2,000m.

Archaeocyathans and stromatoporoids

Two other related fossil groups are the archaeocyathans (around 250 genera known) and stromatoporoids. The archaeocyathans tend to be placed in a class of their own, having evolved and died out during the Cambrian period. Their porous-walled calcareous skeletons closely resemble those of sponges and they may be related or represent a separately evolved sponge-like group. Although the vase-shaped skeletons grew no more than 20cm high, they formed some of the first small reef-like structures known.

The fossil record of stromatoporoids begins in the Ordovician. They are now distributed between the calcisponges and demosponges. They mostly grew as small dome-shaped and layered calcareous mounds, which were important components of Palaeozoic reefs.

Cretaceous oysters have colonized the surface of this fossil sponge

Corals

Corals belong in the phylum Cnidaria, which also includes the jellyfish and sea-anemones. With their calcium carbonate skeletons, the corals have a very important fossil record. The other soft-bodied cnidarians have little in the way of a fossil record except perhaps amongst the Late Precambrian ediacarans of 600 million years ago and very rare preservation in localities such as the Lower Cambrian Chengjiang deposits of China. Today there are altogether some 9,000 cnidarian species, most of which live in the sea. The corals generally live as both solitary and colonial forms on sediment surfaces in warm shallow seas, but some solitary corals can survive in cold deep ocean waters.

Corals build incremental calcium carbonate skeletons up to several metres in size and thus have considerable fossil potential. They are one of the most important fossil groups, with an extensive record extending back into Cambrian times.

The development of coral reefs has been of immense importance to the evolution of marine ecosystems since the Ordovician. Reefs have provided shelter and food for a great diversity of other organisms, from microbes to sharks and turtles. Reefs are the marine equivalents of rainforests and may support as many as a million species of other organisms. Many of their corals are dependent upon light, because their tissues are inhabited by photosynthetic algae.

The Palaeozoic evolution of the corals produced two major groupings, the rugose and tabulate corals, which can be distinguished by certain details of their skeletons, such as the presence of axial structures and bilaterally symmetrical patterning of the blade-like septae in the rugose corals, which are also mostly solitary. In contrast, all tabulates are colonial and have horizontal partitions instead of axial ones. Both groups became extinct during the end-Permian extinction event.

Modern corals are scleractinians and evolved in the Triassic period from a soft coral group that survived the extinction. Their skeletons are composed of the calcium carbonate mineral aragonite rather than the calcite of the Palaeozoic corals. The blade-like septae are radially symmetrical and generally extend right to the outer wall of the coral.

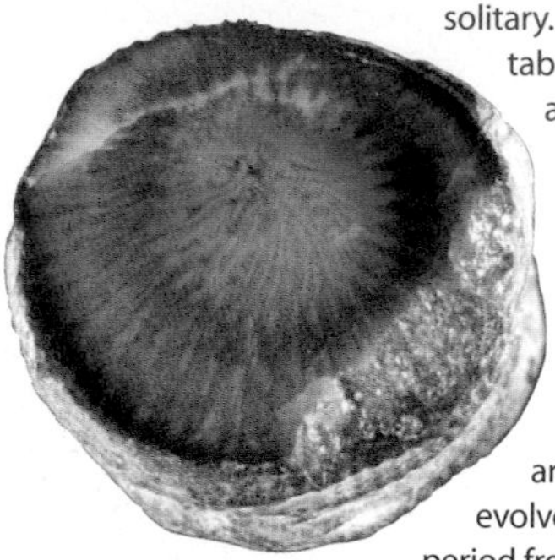

***Dibunophyllum*, a Carboniferous fossil coral, cut to show the septal plates**

Bryozoans (moss animals)

Biologically, these small water-dwelling and filter-feeding colonial animals are much more advanced than corals and are placed in their own phylum (Bryozoa).

Individuals are generally less than 1mm in size, but grow by asexual budding and build centimetre-sized calcium carbonate skeletons that house many thousands of individuals. Their colonies often encrust the surfaces of algae or shells, but some develop as fan-shaped networks and occasionally build more solid three-dimensional forms.

The secretion of mineralized and preservable skeletons by marine bryozoans has resulted in a good fossil record that extends back to the Ordovician. However, several groups became extinct at the end of the Triassic. There are some 6,000 living species, most of which are marine.

***Fenestella*, a Palaeozoic bryozoan (moss animal)**

WORMS AND BURROWS

Palaeontologists tend to lump a motley selection of different soft-bodied organisms together as 'worms', because they have little in the way of a fossil record apart from traces of their activities.

Biologically, such 'worms' belong within a number of phyla such as the annelids, nematodes, platyhelminths, onychophorans, priapulids and so on. Some are fossilized in exceptional circumstances, such as the annelid polychaetes (Cambrian–Recent), priapulids (mostly known as fossils from the Cambrian and Carboniferous but with 17 living species) and onychophorans ('velvet worms', Cambrian–Recent) of the famous Cambrian rock strata of the Burgess Shale in North America and the Chinese Chengjiang deposits.

***Rotularia*, a cluster of serpulid worm tubes**

Being soft-bodied, many 'worms', especially members of the phylum Annelida (with some 15,000 living species), retreat within sediments for protection. They disturb the layering sufficiently to leave distinctive traces of activities such as burrowing and feeding. Such trace fossils are of considerable importance in helping to reconstruct past environments.

There were some tiny, unrelated, tube-shaped animals that did have preservable hard parts. Three of these extinct fossil groups built calcareous cone-shaped shells: the tentaculitids (Ordovician–Carboniferous), cornulitids (Ordovician–Carboniferous) and hyolithids (Cambrian–Permian). Some annelid polychaetes (bristle-worms) are active predators and have tiny preservable organic jaws known as scolecodonts (Ordovician–Present). Others build living-tubes from selected materials such as sand grains or bits of shell and yet others secrete calcareous tubes, which are often coiled and are known as serpulids. Some Cenozoic serpulids, such as *Rotularia*, formed reef-like masses and there are around 500 species alive today.

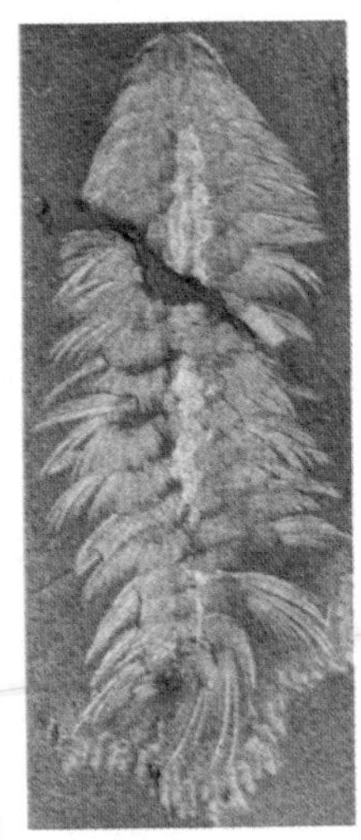

***Canadia*, a Cambrian polychaete (bristleworm)**

BRACHIOPODS

Brachiopods (commonly known as lampshells) are represented by just a hundred or so genera today, but well over 4,000 extinct genera are known. They were common sea-dwelling shelled invertebrates throughout much of Palaeozoic and Mesozoic eras but have decreased in abundance and diversity ever since.

Superficially, brachiopods look like bivalved clams; however, they show important differences and biologically they belong to a quite separate group of animals. Most brachiopods live anchored to the seabed or other surface by a fleshy stalk (called a pedicle).

These shelly invertebrate animals range in size from a millimetre or so up to 20cm and function as simple filter pumps that collect finely particulate organic food from the surrounding seawater. The combined pump and sieve mechanism is a feathery structure (called a lophophore) contained within the shell, so that much of the internal space is filled with water. The other body organs (the gut, muscles and so on) only take up a small part of the interior. The name brachiopod means 'arm-foot' and was given them before it was realized that the lophophore cannot be extended out of the shell.

The brachiopods have not diversified over time nearly as much as the more 'plastic' bivalved molluscs. Nevertheless, within limits, the brachiopods have changed in shape, structure and ornament in response to different lifestyles and environments. For example, in high-energy environments some rhynchonellids have become free-living, the craniids have become cemented to the substrate rather than attached by their pedicle and some terebratulids have short, thick and strong pedicles for survival in powerful currents. On low-energy soft substrates, certain brachiopods have become oyster-like with large flat but thin-walled shells (strophomenids). Productids had spines to support them on soft mud and lingulids used their large pedicles to burrow into the seabed sediments.

The classification of the brachiopods has been reorganized in recent years with the recognition of four main orders (Lingulida, Acrotretida, Rhynchonellida, and Terbratulida) at the subphylum level because there are significant differences in their biology. The main groups can be recognized quite easily with a bit of practice.

***Gibbithyris*, a Cretaceous terebratulid brachiopod**

The earliest brachiopods of Early Cambrian age were linguliforms with shells made of phosphate minerals and organic compounds. They used their large pedicles to burrow in the sediment. As a group they have survived largely unchanged to the present day.

Later in the Cambrian, representatives of both other main groups evolved. However of these, only the Rhynchonelliformea diversified to any great extent into eight separate orders, most of which flourished in Palaeozoic times. Their shells were made of calcium carbonate (calcite) and organic material and were hinged together by teeth and sockets. They were the most common shellfish living in shallow continental-shelf seas around the world, but suffered significant extinctions at the end of the Permian and Triassic periods. Two orders survive: the Rhynchonellida (Ordovician–Recent) and the Terebratulida (Devonian–Recent).

A strophomenid brachiopod of Palaeozoic age

THE MOLLUSCS

The phylum Mollusca is one of the most interesting, diverse and important of invertebrate groups. Today there are some 50,000 species of molluscs and some 60,000 fossil species have been described, most of which are snails and clams. But the phylum also includes several other minor groups such as the shelled chitons (polyplacophorans, Cambrian–Recent), limpet-like monoplacophorans (Cambrian–Recent), extinct snail-like bellerophontids (Cambrian–Triassic), extinct clam-like rostroconchs (Cambrian–Permian) and tusk-shells (scaphopods, Ordovician–Recent). The phylum has, for the most part, an excellent fossil record that extends back to the Cambrian, because so many molluscs build calcareous shells for protection from their numerous predators.

Today, the most familiar shelled molluscs are the clams (Bivalvia, Cambrian–Recent) and snails (Gastropoda, Cambrian–Recent), whose slimy skins and soft fleshy bodies make them so attractive as food for a wide range of animals from crabs to birds and humans. They are found in a wide range of habitats from ocean depths to fresh waters and onto land. They all originated in the sea and gradually spread into fresh waters (in the Devonian). Then, with the evolution of a lung-like structure, a group of snails were able to invade the land in the Cretaceous period.

Just as important is the wide range of sea-dwelling Cephalopoda (Cambrian–Recent), of which the best known today are the squid, cuttlefish and octopus. Less well known are the very few surviving nautiloids, but in the geological past these were very abundant shelled molluscs along with their relatives, the extinct ammonoids. These cephalopods are of great palaeontological interest as their coiled and chambered fossil shells are often abundant. Their rapid evolution and widespread distribution across ancient oceans and seas make them very useful for helping subdivide strata into well defined and temporally constrained biozones and correlate geographically separated strata of similar age.

Biologically, the cephalopods are remarkable animals: they have evolved eyes that in some ways resemble those of a human, and their sight is the most acute among invertebrates, and some, such as the squid *Architeuthis*, have become gigantic,

***Turritella*, a marine snail of Cenozoic (Palaeogene) age**

growing to 18m in length whilst others, such as the octopus, are surprisingly intelligent.

All this diversity from the simple bivalved clam to the sophisticated but rarely fossilized octopus has arisen from the same basic body plan that originated in Early Cambrian or more probably in Late Precambrian times, which was perhaps a small limpet-like creature with a flat muscular foot and protected by a mineralized shell.

Clams (class Bivalvia)

In molluscan clams, the two valves are made of calcium carbonate (aragonite and/or calcite) and hinge together with an organic ligament and muscles. In many clams, interlocking teeth and sockets along the hinge-line help with shell articulation. Typically one valve is the mirror-image of the other and anatomically they lie on the left- and right-hand side of the body. Enclosure of the body by the shell provides a degree of protection from many predators. Consequently, the body is somewhat flattened within the shell and there is no immediately evident 'head' or 'tail'. In order to feed and respire, water has to be drawn into the shell through a siphonal tube by the gills, filtered for food and oxygen and then expelled through another tube. Some primitive clams can feed on organic matter in the sediment, but most are filter feeders.

To move around, many clams use their muscular foot, which first has to extend out of the shell. For this activity the valves have to be opened, which makes it vulnerable to predators. Protection for most is by 'clamming up' – using internal muscles that hold the valves tight together – although some clams escape by burrowing and a few can use water-jet propulsion to scoot away.

There are some 8,000 species of clams living today and with their long evolutionary history extending back to the Cambrian, there must have been many more fossil species. They range in size from a few millimetres up to a metre or so in the living giant clam *Tridacna*. Having mineralized shells, their fossil representation is good, but since the calcium carbonate mineral is aragonite in most cases, which is relatively unstable, many clams are preserved either by calcite, which is more stable, or as sediment moulds.

Four main groups of clams are recognized:

1. The primitive Palaeotaxodonta (Cambrian–Recent), also known as nut shells, nestle in the seabed and feed off fine organic-rich sediment, for example *Nucula*;
2. Pteriomorphia (Ordovician–Recent), many of which are attached to a surface by organic threads known as a byssus (for example, the common edible mussel *Mytilus*) whilst others (for example, the oysters) cement one valve to a substrate;

***Gryphea*, a Mesozoic fossil oyster (pteriomorph bivalved mollusc)**

3. Heteroconcha (Ordovician–Recent) include many burrowers such as the common living razor shells (for example, *Ensis*) and cockles (for example, *Cardium*), as well as the tropical giant clam (*Tridacna*). The rudists (Late Jurassic–Cretaceous) were a strange extinct group of cone-shaped heterodonts, some of which grew to over a metre in size;
4. Anomalodesmata (Ordovician–Recent), marine with global distribution; some nesting, a few cemented, mostly burrowers. For example, *Mya arenaria*, the long-necked clam.

Snails (class Gastropoda)

This extraordinarily successful group of molluscs has some 40,000 species alive today and ranges from the deep sea to fresh waters and many terrestrial environments. Typically, the body is protected by a single spiral shell, but some groups no longer possess shells (for example, the common terrestrial slugs and marine sea-hares). The body has a distinct head and tail separated by a flat muscular creeping foot. The rest of the body is carried above the foot in a coiled mass that extends back into the shell into which the head and foot can also be retracted for protection. Some snails can close the entrance to the shell with a circular operculum.

Snails vary in their size from a few millimetres to half a metre or so and in shape from flat planispiral discs to elongate spindles. The coiling of the shell generates a long internal space while providing a more compact shape for transport. The animal can retract as a result of a quite separate twisting of the internal organs (called torsion) into a figure of eight. As a result the gut and intestines extend into a u-shape from the mouth up into the shell and back out again. The anus opens above the head and the entrance to the mantle cavity in which the respiratory gills are enclosed. Different snail groups have varied resolutions to the problems resulting from this insanitary arrangement.

The feeding habits of snails range from herbivory (plants and algae) to parasitism and active predation of other molluscs and even fish. The snail's mouth is equipped with a tough horny organic structure known as a radula, which can rasp plant material and bore through shell with the aid of enzymes. The adaptability of snails has ensured their evolutionary success, especially when they evolved a lung-like structure that allowed them to leave the water and survive on dry land.

Like many molluscs, the shell is mostly made of the relatively soluble calcium carbonate mineral aragonite, so that much of the extensive fossil record of snails (Cambrian–Recent) consists of sediment moulds or shells in which the aragonite has been replaced by less-soluble calcite.

Six groups are recognized:

1. Patellogastropoda includes the familiar limpets with their wide conical shells made of calcite;
2. Vetigastropoda or 'slit-shells' originated in the Late Cambrian, but are today represented by a single 'living fossil' genus, *Petrotrochus*;
3. Cocculiniformia limpet-like with a secondary respiratory organ, including some deep ocean dwellers;
4. Neritomorpha is of minor importance with few taxa;
5. Caenogastropoda is a major group well represented today by groups such as the cowries, conches, cone-shells, volutes, whelks and periwinkles;

6. Heterobranchia includes two main groups: opisthobranchs and pulmonates. The former includes the shell-less nudibranchs or sea-hares whilst the latter includes the freshwater and terrestrial snails and shell-less slugs. Today there are some 15,000 species of land-living snails.

***Straparollus*, a Carboniferous marine snail**

Squids, cuttlefish, *Nautilus* and octopuses (class Cephalopoda)

There are only some 650 species of cephalopod alive today. They are all sea dwellers and range in size from the 18m-long giant squid (*Architeutis*) down to a tiny octopus species only a few millimetres long. They are the most advanced and intelligent of the molluscs and typically have a distinct head with efficient eyes and a series of arms or tentacles arranged around the mouth, which is armed with a horny beak.

Movement is controlled either by the arms, which are generally equipped with adhesive suckers, or by a water-jet propulsion system. Water is expelled with force from the mantle cavity through a tube called the hyponome and, depending on which direction it is pointed, the animal is propelled rapidly in the opposite direction. Its efficiency also depends upon the relative streamlining of the animal and its shell, if it has one. Squids and cuttlefish are streamlined fast swimmers whilst the Pearly Nautilus with its globose shell is slow.

The octopus does not have a shell and both squid and cuttlefish have a reduced internal shell structure, so none of these cephalopod groups is well represented in the fossil record. However, the nautiloids and ammonoids are cephalopods with coiled and chambered shells that are common as fossils. The chambers are separated by curved walls called septa, through which there is an interconnecting tube called the siphuncle. The chambers are filled with a gas/liquid mixture, whose relative proportions can be altered by the animal. This acts as a buoyancy control mechanism – the more liquid, the deeper the animal sinks in the water column.

Of the shelled cephalopods, only the nautiloids survive, with a few species of the beautiful Pearly Nautilus living in the tropical waters of the Indo-Pacific Ocean. The nautiloids are an ancient group (Late Cambrian–Recent) with numerous fossil forms (around 1,000 genera) that were abundant in Palaeozoic seas. During their evolution the nautiloids evolved from simple straight coned 'orthoconic' forms (for example, *Orthoceras*) to those with tightly coiled shells similar to the living *Nautilus*. *Cameroceras* was an unusual giant orthocone, which grew to some 10m long. During the end-Triassic extinction event, the groups suffered a major setback and only partly recovered in Mesozoic times.

In contrast, the ammonoids became of increasing importance from the Late Palaeozoic but only just survived into the Mesozoic. They first appeared in the Early Devonian and diversified into a number of groups before nearly becoming extinct during the end-Permian extinction event. However, enough survived to recover and flourish during the Mesozoic before finally becoming extinct during the end-Cretaceous extinction event. Their evolution was

***Amaltheus*, a Jurassic ammonite**

marked by increasing complexity of the septal walls between the chambers. They show a much greater variation in shell shape than the nautiloids and were probably adapted for a wider range of habitats from the deep sea to coral reefs and rough shallow waters. Many of them show a marked difference in shell size between the sexes (technically known as sexual dimorphism), with males being much smaller than females. Their rapid evolution and widespread occurrence throughout the world's seas and oceans has made their fossils very important for the biostratigraphic subdivision of marine strata (*see* p.77).

The goniatite ammonoids (for example, *Goniatites*) flourished during the Carboniferous and Permian and were replaced by the ceratites (for example, *Ceratites*) during the Permian and Triassic periods and then the true ammonites (for example, *Hildoceras*, *Amaltheus*, *Scaphites*, *Hoplites*) from the Jurassic to the end of the Cretaceous.

The extinct belemnites were a group of squid-like animals that had an internal shell guard, which is commonly preserved as a bullet-shaped fossil up to 30cm long (for example, *Megateuthis*, *Actinocamax*). Unlike most shelled cephalopods, the belemnite is composed of calcite and thus has considerable fossilization potential. The animals were eaten by extinct marine reptiles such as the ichthyosaurs, and the indigestible mineralized 'guard' was either regurgitated or passed through the digestive system and excreted. The earliest belemnites date from the Early Devonian, but they were most common during the Jurassic and Cretaceous and just survived the end Cretaceous extinction, dying out in early Paleogene times.

ANIMALS WITH JOINTED LEGS (PHYLUM ARTHROPODA)

The huge diversity of the arthropods ranges from tiny living insects such as fleas to giant crustaceans such as spider crabs (with metre-length legs) and extinct Palaeozoic trilobites and eurypterids.

Adaptability is the secret of arthropod success. Their basic body plan has allowed them to conquer most aquatic and terrestrial environments. The body has numerous serially repeated segments and a threefold division into head, thorax and abdomen, to which several pairs of jointed legs and other appendages (varying from antennae, jaws and wings to gills) are attached. In addition the body and limbs are protected by a tough organic 'armour' (exoskeleton), which is mineralized in some groups such as the crustaceans. The exoskeleton not only protects the body parts but provides a semi-rigid surface for attachment of the muscles that move the limbs. The only drawback is that for growth the exoskeleton has to be periodically discarded and replaced, which makes the animal vulnerable to predation until the new, larger exoskeleton has hardened.

Arguably, arthropods are one of the most successful groups of animals of all time, with a long evolutionary history stretching back to earliest Cambrian times and probably into Late Precambrian times. They originated in marine waters and were the first animals to colonize fresh waters in the Ordovician and dry land by the Early Silurian, and they were the first to fly in the Carboniferous period (dragonflies). Today, whilst many arthropods are serious pests, others are essential parts of the ecosystem, either directly or indirectly through their role as pollinators of food plants.

The fossil record of the arthropods is quite patchy: groups that have mineralized exoskeletons, such as the trilobites, crabs and ostracods, are much better represented than those with thin organic exoskeletons such as the insects. Nevertheless, many ancient sediments have now been found that preserve depositional environments with fossilized insects and otherwise rare arthropods. Thanks to ancient Cambrian deposits, such as those of Chengjiang in China and the Burgess Shale in Canada, the arthropods' early evolution and diversification is now better understood. Similarly, deposits such as those of Devonian age at Rhynie in Scotland, and several amber deposits around the world of Jurassic to Cenozoic age, reveal a great deal about the evolution and diversification of insects.

Classification of the arthropods is much debated, but four or five major groups are generally recognized:

- The extinct trilobitomorphs (Cambrian–Permian);
- The chelicerates: a large group with a carapace divided into a prosoma with pincers and an opisthosoma with an extended tail, such as the

horseshoe crabs, eurypterids, scorpions and spiders (Cambrian–Recent);

- The crustaceans, many of which have mineralized exoskeletons, such as crabs, shrimps, lobsters, ostracods, barnacles, woodlice and the extinct phyllocarids (Cambrian–Recent);
- The uniramians, with limbs that have a single branch, include myriapods such as the centipedes and millipedes (Ordovician–Recent);
- The insects, with their extraordinary abundance and diversity, such as cockroaches, dragonflies, ants, beetles, wasps and flies (Silurian–Recent).

Trilobites

Trilobites are one of the most famous extinct fossil groups, with some 15,000 species known. The repeated shedding of the mineralized exoskeletons during growth of the individual animal has ensured an excellent representation of the group in the fossil record. They were all marine and mostly seabed dwellers, but some were capable of swimming and have widespread oceanic distributions.

Most trilobites have flattened bodies that range in size from a millimetre or so up to 72cm and are protected by their mineralized exoskeleton on the upper side. The name trilobite refers to the longitudinal division of the exoskeleton into three lobes. The strongly convex axis down the centre is the axial lobe; the two more flattened regions on either side of it are the pleural lobes, each separated from the axial lobe by an axial furrow. The exoskeleton is also divided transversely, into the celaphon (head), thorax (body) and pygidium (tail). The head consists of three solid plates, and the body has a number of interlocking and flexible segments that allow many trilobites to roll up into a defensive ball; in this position, the single tail plate is curled under the head and protects the vulnerable underside of the animal.

***Dalmanites*, a phacopid trilobite of Silurian age**

The first trilobites appear in the Early Cambrian evolutionary 'explosion', which includes a great diversity of arthropods. Presumably they had Late Precambrian ancestors whose remains have not yet been found or recognized. Their heyday was from Late Cambrian through the Ordovician; they still flourished during the Devonian but subsequently declined, finally becoming extinct during the end-Permian extinction event.

The trilobites are subdivided into nine orders:

1. Agnostida (Early Cambrian–Late Ordovician), small forms, for example *Eodiscus*;

2. Redlichiida (Early–Middle Cambrian), primitive forms, often spiny, for example *Olenellus*;
3. Corynexochida (Early Cambrian–Late Devonian), forms with ten or less thoracic segments, for example *Bumastus*;
4. Ptychopariida (Early Cambrian–Late Devonian), varied group, for example *Elrathia*;
5. Harpetida (Late Cambrian–Late Devonian), forms with small eyes, for example *Eoharpes*;
6. Proetida (Late Cambrian–Late Permian), includes last trilobites, for example *Phillipsia*;
7. Phacopida (Early Ordovician–Late Devonian), varied forms, for example *Dalmanites*;
8. Lichida (Middle Cambrian–Late Devonian), covered with tubercles, for example *Odontopleurida*;
9. Asaphida (Middle Cambrian–Late Silurian), smooth forms, for example *Asaphus*.

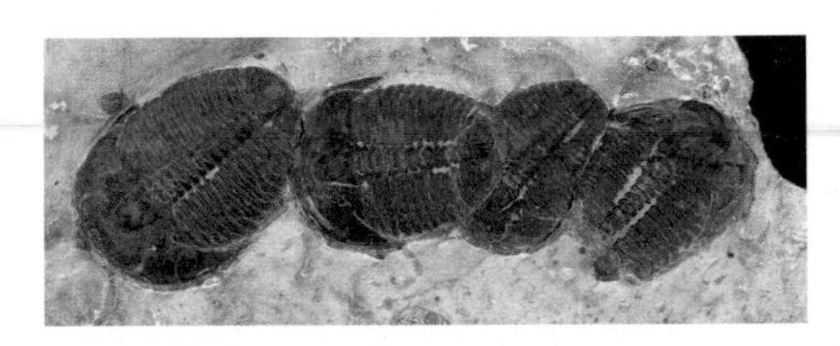

***Elrathia*, a small Cambrian trilobite from Utah, USA**

Chelicerates

The chelicerates are a huge group of some 65,000 living species. They range from the extinct eurypterids to the 'living fossil' horseshoe crabs and the more familiar spiders (arachnids) and mites. They are distinguished from other arthropods by the twofold division of the body and the pair of pincers developed from the first segment, which are well seen in the scorpions.

Horseshoe crabs (xiphosurans), whose fossil record extends back into the Cambrian, are represented by four living species that look superficially like some trilobites. More important are the eurypterids, which include *Pterygotus*, the largest known arthropod of Silurian– Devonian age, which grew to over 2.3m long. With large pincers, eurypterids were top predators in both marine and fresh waters.

The arachnids include not just the familiar spiders but also mites, ticks and scorpions. Most live on land and can breathe air through use of a structure called a 'book-lung'. The earliest fossil arachnids appear in Upper Silurian strata and, although their record is patchy, some lake deposits and amber have preserved a number of fossils.

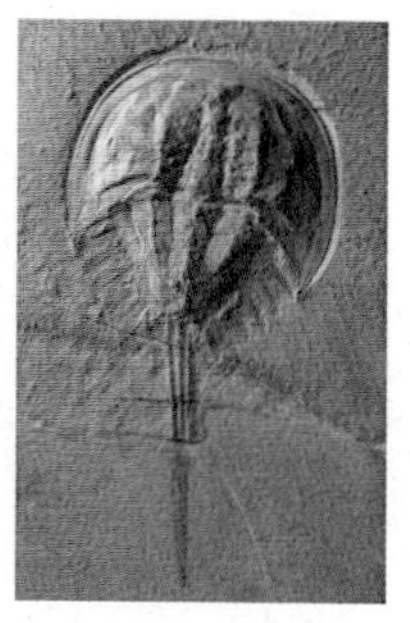

A fossil xiphosuran

Crustaceans

This is another large group of important arthropods, with some 50,000 living species with a good fossil record thanks to the mineralization of the exoskeleton. Crabs, lobsters, shrimps, barnacles, crayfish and woodlice are all familiar living crustaceans that occupy many aquatic and terrestrial environments.

Less familiar are the ostracods and phyllocarids, but both are important in the history of life, especially the ostracods. The latter are small (1–10mm long) shrimp-like animals whose bodies are enclosed in a bivalved and mineralized shell. Their remains are commonly preserved in many seabed and some freshwater sediments. The phyllocarids form a group of Palaeozoic (Ordovician–Recent) abundant shrimp-like crustaceans (for example *Ceratiocaris*). Like all arthropod groups, the crustaceans originated in the sea and have a long history extending back into the Cambrian period.

Uniramians

This major group of the arthropods includes the myriapods, containing the familiar land-living millipedes and centipedes with their numerous body segments and pairs of legs. There are Ordovician trackways that were possibly made by myriapods. If so, these were probably the first animals to venture out of

***Procambarus*, a 50-million-year-old fossil crustacean crayfish, from Wyoming, USA**

the sea into terrestrial fresh waters; by the Silurian, fossil remains (for example *Pneumodesmus*) show they had gained a foothold on dry land. Typically, they eat rotting vegetation and, in the Carboniferous forests, giant myriapods such as *Arthropleura* grew to 2m in length.

Insects

One of the most spectacular groups of animals, there are nearly a million known species of insect alive today including 300,000 beetles. Altogether there may be as many as 5 million species. With a fossil record extending back to the Devonian, their potential fossil diversity is immense. However, because their exoskeleton is not mineralized, their fossilization potential is low. Only certaln sediments, such as lake and lagoon muds and amber, preserve insects. Nevertheless, some 40,000 species of fossil insect have been described.

The insect body has three parts: a head with six segments, a thorax with three, and an abdomen with 11 or fewer. The head has sensory antennae, chewing mandibles and compound eyes. Typically there are two pairs of wings on the body and each body segment has a pair of walking legs. However, there have been many departures from this basic plan, and insects have colonized almost all terrestrial environments and many aquatic ones.

There are some spectacular fossil insects, such as *Meganeura*, a giant dragonfy with a 70cm wingspan, and *Archimylacris*, a 9cm-long cockroach. Both lived in the Carboniferous Coal Measure forests. Many insects are highly specialized and they have played an enormously important role in plant evolution. Many are also adapted to particular climate conditions. Consequently, their remains are very useful in the reconstruction of past climates, especially those of the Pleistocene ice ages.

An insect preserved in Dominican amber

ECHINODERMS

As their name implies, the echinoderms are a group (phylum) of animals with spiny 'skins', which includes the familiar and abundant sea urchins and starfish that live in shallow seas today. However, the group also includes the sea-lilies (crinoids), brittle-stars (ophiuroids) and sea-cucumbers (holothurians). Altogether there are some 6,000 living species as well as a number of extinct groups.

Biologically this is a fascinating group, many of whose members have a unique body geometry showing a fivefold (pentaradial) symmetry as adults, so there is no obvious head or tail. Consequently, they do not look like animals and some (for example, sea-lilies) seem strangely plantlike. And yet many of them are mobile, using a unique hydraulic powered water vascular system of extensible tube feet to get about, or even muscle-powered spines in the case of the sea urchins. The tube feet are also variously used for respiration, feeding and chemoreception. The echinoderms have advanced larval features that relate them to the chordates.

The skeleton looks superficially like an exoskeleton or shell, especially in the sea urchins, but is actually a more sophisticated structure. It is commonly made up of many porous calcareous plates filled with tissue, which also forms a thin covering to the 'shell' and holds it together. In the starfish and sea cucumbers the calcareous skeleton is reduced to small spicules embedded in the tissue. Upon death the skeleton of many echinoderms falls apart as the tissue rots. The individual plates become scattered within the seabed sediment and are a common component of many 'shelly' limestones. However, entire fossils of sea urchins (apart from their spines, which easily fall off) and sea-lilies can be found.

The echinoderm way of life varies enormously from the sedentary sea-lilies, which live rooted to a surface and filter small organic particles from the surrounding seawater, to the carnivorous starfish that are very effective in hunting down and attacking molluscan clams. The starfish pull the clams open with their arms and evert their stomachs between the victim's shells to then digest the flesh.

We know a great deal about their long history, extending back into Cambrian times, thanks to the common preservation of their calcareous (calcite) skeletons. There are a number of extinct fossil groups that lived during Palaeozoic times, such as the cystoids, blastoids, edrioasteroids, amongst others. The echinoderms are classified into five main groups (subphyla):

1. The Echinozoa (Early Cambrian–Recent) with globe- or disc-shaped radiate skeletons and include the sea urchins, sea cucumbers and the extinct edrioasteroideans;

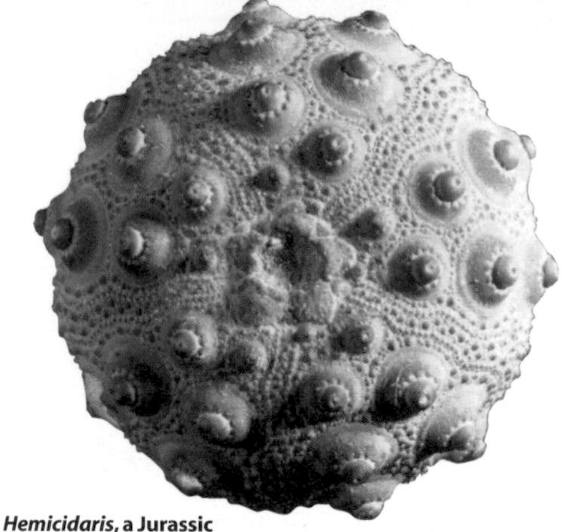

***Hemicidaris*, a Jurassic echinoid whose spines have not been preserved**

2. The Asterozoa (Ordovician–Recent) have disc-shaped bodies and five or more arms and include the starfish and brittle stars;
3. The Crinozoa (Mid Cambrian–Recent), the sea-lilies with food-gathering arms attached to a small plated body and fixed stem;
4. The Blastozoa (Early Cambrian–Permian) are filter-feeders with cup-shaped bodies and are often stalked but lack arms; they include the cystoids and other primitive groups;

5. The Homalozoa another curious extinct group (Cambrian–Devonian), which includes the mitrates, cornutes and solutes. They possess a skeleton made of echinoderm-like calcareous plates but lack their pentaradial symmetry. Instead they are curiously asymmetric with a theca (head/body) to which a flexible tail and a few arm-like appendages are attached. There has been a long running argument as to whether these are actually chordate rather than echinoderm-related animals. Recent finds indicate that they are indeed echinoderms.

***Coranguinum*, a Cretaceous burrowing echinoid (sea urchin)**

UNUSUAL FOSSILS

Graptolites

The name graptolite means 'rock writing', and many fossils of this extinct and largely Early Palaeozoic group do look like little more than graphitic pencil lines on rock surfaces. However, they are an important group with considerable palaeontological interest.

The graptolites were colonial invertebrate animals and abundant in ancient seas, from the Silurian to Early Devonian. The graptolites were made of asexually produced and interconnected small zooids, up to several hundred in some species. Each zooid was only a millimetre or so in size but they were linked together into threadlike and often branched networks, some of which stretched up to a metre in length. The animals were filter feeders and it is probable that each zooid was armed with two small feathery tentacles for trapping small organic particles.

The zooids built an organic skeleton to house the colony and it is the carbonized remains of the skeleton that comprises the graptolite fossil. The dendroid graptolites grew into small bushy colonies up to 10cm high. However, the majority of graptoloid graptolites (*see* classification below) were free-living, abundant and widely distributed within ancient seas. Like the ammonites of the Mesozoic, graptolites also evolved rapidly and have long been recognized as

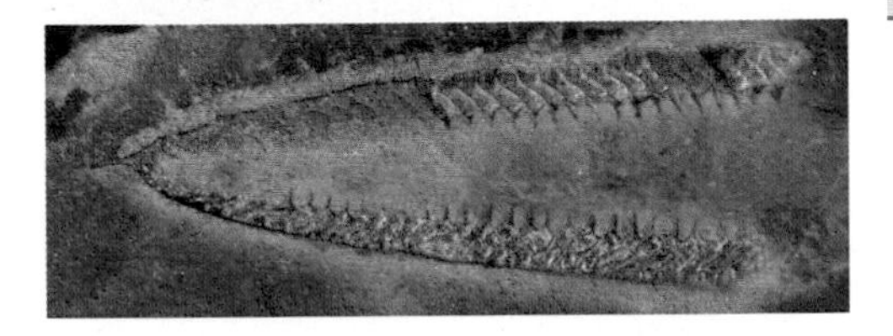

***Didymograptus*, an Ordovician graptolite, some 465 million years old**

extremely useful in the biostratigraphic subdivision of Lower Palaeozoic strata. Many graptolite biozones had durations of around a million years.

The living pterobranchs are a minor group of marine colonial animals that have a free-swimming tadpole-like larva and adults that live attached to a surface. Their biology places them in the hemichordate phylum and they build organic skeletons with features similar to graptolites. Consequently, the graptolites are generally seen as a group of extinct hemichordates.

In terms of classification, the class Graptolithina (Middle Cambrian–Late Carboniferous) is divided into two major groups and some seven minor ones: the largely sessile dendroids (Middle Cambrian–Late Carboniferous, for example *Dictyonema*) and the free-living graptoloids (Ordovician–Early Devonian, for example *Didymograptus*, *Monograptus*).

Conodonts

Conodonts, or 'cone teeth', are a group of sea-dwelling animals that is of great interest to palaeontologists. The biological affinities of these tiny (1–4mm, rarely up to 15mm long) fossil tooth-like elements were one of the great fossil puzzles for over a century, because no other part of the animal was found.

The elements are mineralized with calcium phosphate (apatite) and the fossils are found in Cambrian to Triassic limestones, from which they are extracted by chemical means. Many of the tooth-like elements consist of sharp spikes growing from a bar, but others are flatter, platform-like structures.

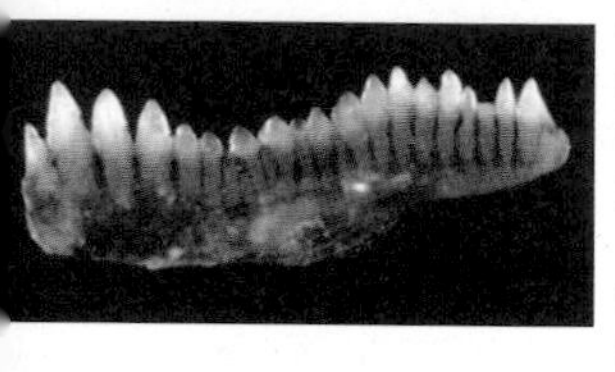

Spathognatodus, one part of the feeding apparatus of an Early Carboniferous age conodont animal from Iowa, USA

The elements occur in mirror-image pairs, several of which formed the feeding apparatus of these tiny, free-swimming, eel-shaped predators (10–50mm long), whose chordate anatomy was very close to the vertebrates. Giant Ordovician conodont animals up to half a metre long have been found in South Africa.

Their wide distribution and rapid evolution make conodonts important for biostratigraphy.

MICROFOSSILS

The study of fossils (palaeontology) is divided into a number of broad areas of expertise, such as fossil plants (palaeobotany), vertebrates, invertebrates, trace fossils (palaeoichnology) and small fossils in general (micropalaeontology). The last includes a vast array of fossil remains from a huge diversity of organisms, such as single-celled plants, fungi, small animals such as ostracods or small parts of large animals such as conodonts. Consequently, micropalaeontology is further subdivided into areas of specialization such as the study of plant pollen (palynology), small vertebrate remains (mostly teeth) and so on.

Most amateur fossil hunters just collect the fossils that they can see in rock strata, in other words those remains that are visible to the eye and are generally greater than 2mm in size. These are sometimes referred to as 'macrofossils' to distinguish them from the smaller 'microfossils'. Even so, the smaller of these macrofossils are best seen with a hand lens. Beyond the resolution of the eye the other world of microfossils can only be seen with a microscope. They generally require special extractive techniques, such as the dissolution of the rock matrix with acid.

Of this diversity of microfossils only a sample can be dealt with here. It includes the shells of single-celled (protistan) animals known as foraminifers (forams for short) and acritarchs, plant spores and pollen (palynology). Other interesting and important groups include radiolarians (marine microplanktonic animals), diatoms and coccolithophores (single-celled plantlike organisms) and small fish-related structures such as scales and teeth.

Foraminifers

Foraminifers are shelled unicellar organisms, which are grouped together with familiar naked forms (such as amoebas) as sarcodines. They have a long fossil history extending back to the Cambrian and probably even earlier into Late Precambrian times. Biologically, they are a very interesting group and in recent decades their fossils have become particularly important as proxy measures of past climate change.

It is remarkable that a single cell can build a mineralized and chambered spiral shell as it grows. Most are just a millimetre or so in size but some giants (the nummulites) grew into coin-like discs up to 60mm in diameter. The shells are either calcareous and made of calcite or agglutinated masses of shell fragments or sand grains.

Both seabed dwelling (benthic) and near surface (planktonic) forms are known and they may be incredibly abundant in nutrient-rich tropical waters, so much so that some modern deep ocean 'ooze' deposits are made almost entirely of foram shells. Recovery of such deposits laid down over the last few million years has allowed the proxy measure of climate change through analysis of the isotopic composition of foram shells. This work has been fundamental to the realization that climates can change rapidly and frequently, especially over the last 5 million or so years with the successive ice ages.

The earliest forams are agglutinated forms of Early Cambrian age, and it was not until the Devonian that calcitic shelled forms evolved. A considerable diversity was achieved by the Carboniferous period and they were abundant enough to be used as biostratigraphic markers in limestones of this age.

Giant protistan nummulites (foraminiferans) of Eocene age from Egypt

Acritarchs, plant spores and pollen (palynology)

There is a vast range of organic walled microfossils, with a fossil record extending right back into Precambrian times. Indeed, they include some of the oldest evidence of life, the remains of prokaryotic cyanobacteria that probably built stromatolitic sediment mounds in shallow warm seas from around 3.5 billion years ago (*see* p.37). Fossilization of some of these microbes (filaments and cyst-like bodies) has occurred in certain exceptional circumstances (for example, the 3.5 billion-year-old Apex Chert of Western Australia and the 2 billion-year-old Gunflint Chert of Ontario, Canada).

The evolution of sea-dwelling eukaryotic micro-organisms around 1,200 million years ago produced a new diversity of groups ranging from fungi and red algae to the first multicelled organisms (metazoans). Many of these produced microscopically small and tough organic-walled cyst stages during their life cycles and these are generally referred to as acritarchs. From the Late Precambrian through the Palaeozoic, some 500 genera of fossil acritarchs have been recognized and many of their species have biostratigraphical use even though their taxonomic relationships are not known.

Spores and pollen are organic-walled and microscopic parts of the plant reproductive system. Fossil spores and pollen are mostly derived from land plants with the former being mostly less than 200 microns in diameter (although some megaspores are of millimetre size) whilst the latter are smaller at between 2 and 150 microns. They are generally adapted to be extremely durable and capable of surviving desiccation, oxidation, ultra-violet light, abrasion and transport by wind and water. As a result they are commonly trapped, buried and fossilized in many sedimentary environments both on land and in near-shore marine deposits. Their recovery from rock strata often involves pretty brutal treatment with a variety of powerful acids. Surprisingly, these tiny fossils often survive such treatment and emerge with delicate structures intact.

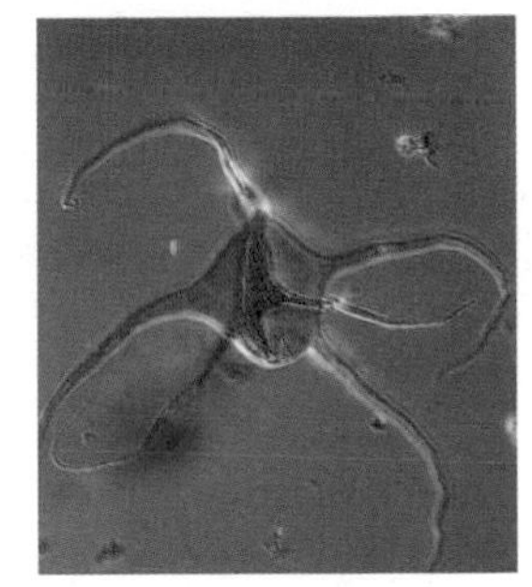

Microscopic acritarch from Silurian marine strata

The recovery of large numbers of identifiable spores and pollen, even from small chips of rock derived from drill holes, has been of great importance in the investigation of hydrocarbon-bearing rock strata. Consequently, there has been detailed study of the biostratigraphic potential of these microfossils and all other microfossil groups showing such potential. The identification of plant pollen from Neogene sediments has greatly assisted our understanding of the changing climates and environments of the most recent ice age, because so many plants are climate sensitive.

Many of these microfossils are named and classified according to their external morphology without the identity of the parent plant being known. Only those related to living plant species and groups can be placed in their appropriate 'parental' categories.

The earliest spores derived from land plants are found in Ordovician strata and probably belong to moss-like bryophytes. True vascular land plants (*see* p.86) did not evolve until early in the Silurian, and from then on spores diversified enormously.

A Late Devonian progymnosperm plant frond from Kiltorcan, Ireland

THE FOSSIL RECORD: PLANTS

Plants, like animals, are eukaryotic organisms in which each cell has a membrane-bound nucleus. But plants and algae, unlike animals, also possess chloroplasts that allow them to use carbon dioxide and light energy from the Sun to build complex organic molecules that form their body tissues. A by-product of this photosynthetic process is oxygen.

Thus algae and plants have been essential to the evolution of life-supporting environments on Earth. In early Precambrian times, photosynthesizing micro-organisms that lived in shallow seas and ocean surface waters were instrumental in building oxygen levels in both the oceans and the atmosphere. Their existence is recorded by fossil stromatolites (*see* p.37) and a variety of organic walled microfossils in Precambrian strata around the world (for example, the 2 billion-year-old Gunflint Chert, Ontario, Canada).

These same primitive micro-organisms were food for the first multicelled animals in the oceans. Marine waters were also home to the first large green algae, whose frond-like growths are so familiar in coastal and many fresh waters today.

THE FIRST LAND PLANTS

The increasing abundance of fossil spores in the Lower Palaeozoic sedimentary rock record and the development of the first soils shows that primitive moss-like (bryophyte) plants may have pioneered life on land during the Ordovician. The following Silurian period saw the evolution of the more advanced vascular plants and the invertebrate animal communities that depended upon them.

Pioneering life on land was as difficult for plants as it was for animals. In the absence of the supportive and protective medium of water, the oxidizing and dehydrating effects of a light gaseous atmosphere and the influence of gravity were powerful and damaging. Plant tissues had to be strengthened to grow up from the ground surface and carry water-based nutrients from the soil through rootlike structures to the highest extremities of the plant by means of a plumbing system. The surface tissues (the cuticle) had to be protected against damaging sun-rays and dehydration and yet also be porous enough to allow the exchange of gases from the air into the plant cells.

Fossils of some of the earliest of these so-called vascular plants (for example, *Cooksonia*) are known from Silurian strata in Ireland and Britain. They are tiny leafless plants only a few millimetres high with simple forked stems terminated by lobe-shaped spore-containing structures called sporangia. The plants were dependent upon water for reproduction, with male gametes swimming to fertilize the female ones. But they also used wind for the dispersal of their spores (reproductive cells).

From Early to Middle Devonian times vascular plants increased in height to several metres, with more complex branching. For instance, the Middle Devonian Gilboa forest in New York had tree-sized plants that grew to 7m high. There is fossil evidence from a freshwater bog-like deposit, called the Rhynie Chert, in Scotland that the 'arms race' between plants and plant-eating animals had already begun. Fossil lesions show that these primitive plants were having to protect themselves from attack by small, sap-sucking arthropods. By the Late Devonian, the first treelike plants with woody tissues, fern-like foliage and reproduction by spores (the progymnosperms, for example *Archaeopteris*) had evolved.

Early Carboniferous times saw the appearance of the first representatives of many of the main plant groups, but these have few survivors today because, as we shall see, modern plants are dominated by the flowering plants (angiosperms), of which the first known appeared in the Early Cretaceous.

The clubmosses (lycopsids, Late Silurian–Recent)

These primitive plants typically have simple stems that grow upright from a horizontal rootlike underground portion. The leaf-like structures (technically known as microphylls) are strap-shaped and arranged helically around the upright stem. Their first fossil representatives in the Late Silurian (for example *Barangwanathia* from Australia) grew only to half a metre or so in height. Reproduction was still through water with spores produced in sporangia attached to the base of the microphylls on their upper surface.

The group diversified during the Devonian and by the Carboniferous they dominated much of the world's vegetation with genera such as *Lepidodendron* growing into giant tree-sized plants some 30m high.

Although they survived the end-Permian extinction event, by the end of the Triassic their diversity was falling and never recovered. Today, there are only a few small genera such as *Selaginella* and the quillwort *Isoetes*.

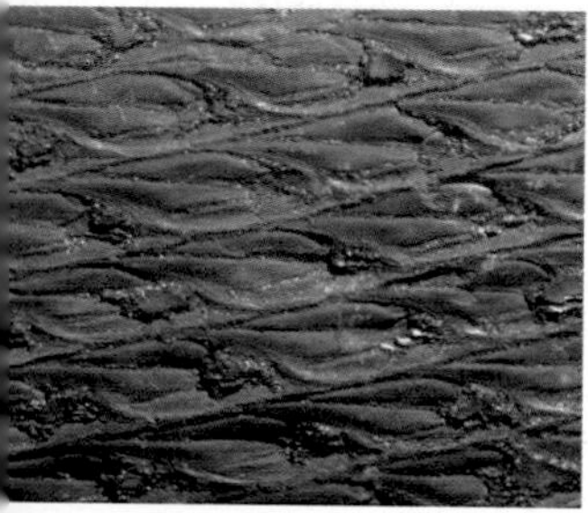

***Lepidodendron*, a Carboniferous lycopsid (clubmoss) stem with leaf scars**

Horsetails (sphenopsids, Late Devonian–Recent)
The horsetails are another group of primitive plants restricted to wet environments and that reproduce by means of spores. They have true roots as well as a horizontal rootlike rhizome from which upright stems grow. The stems have a very distinctive form with narrow and stiff bristly branches arranged in whorls along the stem, which has a jointed appearance.

A stem fragment of *Calamites*, a Carboniferous sphenopsid (horsetail)

The horsetails also have a history of success that parallels that of the clubmosses. Their maximum diversity in the Carboniferous saw the development of some giant tree-sized species such as *Calamites*, which grew to 40m high. This was followed by a continuous decline so that there are some 18 species remaining alive today, all belonging to the genus *Equisetum*.

Ferns (Late Devonian–Recent)

Another group that reproduces by means of spores, the ferns, originated in the Late Devonian. With their frond-shaped leaves with clusters of sporangia on the lower surface, they are much more familiar today than either the clubmosses or horsetails. Indeed the ferns are by far the largest group of seedless vascular plants alive today. Their distinctive flat foliage with leaves that are often intricately divided, makes them very efficient solar panels. They can collect enough light for survival even in the gloom of a forest floor overshadowed by a dense canopy from much larger tree-sized plants. They also have a well-developed root system, which has allowed some of them to succeed as deciduous plants and grow in regions with seasonal climates.

The delicate frond of a Carboniferous fern

The ferns show considerable variation in shape and size, from those with a small rootlike stem (rhizome) that sits on or even under the soil surface to others that form the so-called tree-ferns (from the Late Devonian). These tree-ferns have trunks made up from intertwined roots and stems. Some ferns have become vine-like climbers whose long fronds cling to other plants, and yet other ferns have become water dwelling with fronds that float on the surface of lakes and ponds.

Pteridosperms (Carboniferous-?Recent)

The pteridosperms evolved from a plant group called progymnosperms, with fern-like fronds and reproduction plus conifer-like wood. This structure was elaborated in pteridosperms by expanding the 'female spores' and retaining them within a sporangium and then partially enclosing them in the sporophyll to generate a functional seed. The protected seed, with its own food supply, was a major innovation in plant evolution. But unlike angiosperms, the female sporangium of seed ferns was not wholly enclosed. The seed is said to be 'naked', thus defining a highly diverse group called the gymnosperms of which the seed ferns are the earliest.

They give rise separately to more evolved surviving groups: the cycads, Ginkgo, conifers and gnetaleans, and the angiosperms. Relationships among these groups, and with fossil groups such as corystosperms,

The leaf of a Triassic 'seed fern', *Glossopteris*, from Australia

glossopterids, bennettites, and Caytonia, are highly contentious. DNA evidence conflicts with their fossil record and makes it hard to pinpoint when a plant is no longer a seed fern but belongs to a descendent group. For example, cycads may be living seed ferns. Thus, seed ferns are not a natural group, but they have immense evolutionary significance.

During the Carboniferous, seed ferns became increasingly dominant members of the vegetation. The replacement was probably speeded up by the climate change and their competitive advantage over free-sporing plants that were much more vulnerable to the elements. The gymnosperms flourished throughout the Early Mesozoic (Triassic-Jurassic) and then declined when the more advanced seed-producing and flowering plants began to dominate.

The Carboniferous 'coal measure' forests

Although the first woods and forests were of Late Devonian age, the most extensive developments first occurred in the Carboniferous. It is possible that this extensive tropical vegetation withdrew so much carbon dioxide from the atmosphere and locked it up in plant matter that global climate changed from a greenhouse into icehouse state, with the formation of polar icecaps by the end of the Carboniferous.

The accumulating plant debris formed the first coal deposits, which humans exploited to fuel the Industrial Revolution in Europe and North America. Within a century or so, from the late 18th century through the 19th century, huge volumes of Carboniferous coal measures were mined and burned to stoke the fires of industrialization.

The so-called 'coal-measure' deposits were laid down in low-lying swampy environments associated with lakes, rivers, deltas and flat coastal plains. The clubmosses, horsetails, ferns and seed ferns that flourished at this time were all dependent upon water for reproduction and so were largely restricted to low-lying swampy regions. Nevertheless, the development of woody tissues in the clubmosses and horsetails allowed some of them to grow into 30m-high trees with extensive canopies. Preservation of the stumps of such trees in coal deposits (such as at Joggins in Nova Scotia) shows that these were dense forests.

The forests were rooted in soils on which leaf litter, fallen trunks and branches, along with the remains of their animal inhabitants, from insects to early amphibians and reptiles, accumulated. Where there was regional subsidence, the deposits gradually built up over millions of years. Because they were sealed off from oxygen and did not decay, accumulations were sometimes hundreds of metres thick. More often, layers of plant debris were flooded and swamped by sediment. As a result, coal seams alternate with sandstone or limestone strata containing fossils of water-dwelling creatures from clams to fish and occasionally tadpole larvae of the

Leaf fronds of *Williamsonia*, a Jurassic bennettitalean

amphibians. The resulting deposits frequently show repeated cycles of soils (called seat-earths), coals and sandstones or limestones.

Bennettitaleans (Middle Triassic–Late Cretaceous)
These cycad-like plants produced clusters of seeds in cone-like structures that were sometimes protected by scale-like structures or bracts (for example, *Williamsonia*). Fossils of their leaves can be very difficult to tell apart from cycad leaves and microscopic detail is required to make the distinction.

Cycads (Permian–Recent)
The cycads are yet another group of ancient plants that were much more abundant in the Mesozoic and have just managed to survive into the present. Like the bennettitaleans they reproduced by means of seeds grouped together as cone-like structures borne on fronds. The sexes are separate, with the males producing pollen from their cones. These innovations helped the cycads dominate global vegetation during the relatively dry environments of the Permian and Triassic.

Although modern cycads are restricted to frost-free regions of the world, their fossil record shows that they were much more widely distributed. During the Mesozoic they even grew in polar regions when there were no ice caps but the conditions were still cold, dark and frosty. These ancient cycads had vine-like stems and were deciduous, unlike their modern counterparts such as *Cycas*. This latter genus has whorls of leathery evergreen fronds growing from a squat trunk and its seed-bearing fronds are separate from one another and do not form cones.

Conifers (Carboniferous–Present)

The conifers are the one remaining major group of plants that has an ancient history stretching way back

Leaflet whorls of *Calamites*, a Carboniferous lycopsid

Into the Carboniferous. Although conifers are common plants today that typically form woody trees, they were more diverse and abundant during their Mesozoic heyday.

Conifers reproduce by means of seeds borne on the surface of cone scales, with male and female cones usually growing on the same plant although they are on separate plants in some genera. Some conifer cones are modified to form attractive fleshy and berry-like structures as in the familiar living junipers. More typical female cones have seeds borne on woody scales with tongue-shaped bracts whilst the male, pollen-bearing cones are much smaller and less conspicuous. Fossil pollen and wood from conifers is relatively common in the rock record, especially in alluvial, terrestrial and shallow coastal strata of Mesozoic age.

The plants the dinosaurs ate

Early land-living vertebrates were all flesh-eaters and herbivorous vertebrates did not make much impact on plant life until the Permian. Only subsequently were they abundant and big enough to cause significant damage to vegetation. The study of fossil teeth shows that during the Permian at least eight different groups of vertebrate flesh-eaters evolved plant-eating lineages. It is much more difficult to extract the food value from plants than from flesh and requires very different teeth. Plant matter has to be crushed by the cheek teeth rather than simply chopped up into pieces that are small enough to be swallowed.

The evolution of large-scale plant eating coincided with the rise of the seed plants during the Mesozoic era (Triassic–Cretaceous) and their occupation of seasonally dry areas. To survive such dry conditions the foliage of cycads and conifers had to adapt and become tougher. Consequently, it was also more difficult for the plant-eaters to digest. Another important development (originating in the Devonian) was the production of an outer layer of secondary thickening of plant stems, which allowed the more advanced seed plants to grow higher, thicker and produce well-branched light-gathering canopies.

***Triceratops*, a Late Cretaceous age ceratopsid from Wyoming, USA**

With many plants growing into tall trees, their foliage was more difficult to reach for the relatively small (metre-sized) Permian vertebrate browsers. However, by the Mesozoic the evolution of a new group of reptiles, the dinosaurs, carried the 'arms race' with the plants to a new level of intensity.

From the Late Triassic through into the Late Jurassic, the evolution of the sauropods produced the most formidable individual plant-eaters of all time. With increasingly long necks these browsers were able to reach higher and higher, perhaps up to 12m, into tree crowns to feed. It has been estimated that an adult *Brachiosaurus* ate around 200kg of plants a day. However, without specialized teeth, they had to rely on gut bacteria and swallowed stones that acted as gastric mills to process their plant food.

Different groups of herbivores evolved more effective and specialized tooth forms for processing different plant foods. For example, ornithischians (such as *Triceratops*) had sharp horny beaks for effective cropping of plants, and cheek teeth that were variously adapted for cutting and grinding (as in *Iguanodon*).

The plants produced a number of defensive adaptations such as the tough leaves of cycads along with a build up of toxins in the foliage and seeds. Some araucarian conifers also have very tough leaves that develop along the branches as a spiny barrier, as seen in the living 'monkey puzzle' trees, *Araucaria*.

The other group of dinosaur relatives that began to have a huge impact upon plant life from the Early Cretaceous were the birds. A chicken-sized fossil bird (*Jeholornis prima*) from Lower Cretaceous lake deposits in China has been found with over 50 fossil fruits or seeds (*c.* 9mm wide) preserved within its stomach. This bird was capable of flight and its seed-eating habit also provided a means of dispersal for the plant seeds, since they would have been excreted undamaged. The dinosaur plant-eaters also provided opportunities for the plants they ate by aiding seed dispersal, and they may have inadvertently encouraged the growth of new understorey plants where they fed.

Flowering plants (angiosperms, Jurassic–Recent)

The vegetation of today's landscapes is dominated by flowering plants of remarkable abundance and diversity, ranging from grasses to trees – altogether some 250,000 species grouped into some 450 families. They are probably far more diverse than any other group of plants and have achieved this in a relatively short period of time since the end of the Cretaceous and the eclipse of the Mesozoic cycads, bennettitaleans and conifers. Not since the Late Devonian and Early Carboniferous has there been such a rapid radiation of new kinds of plants.

There are a number of features that are characteristic of flowering plants, but not all flowering plants possess them and some of these characteristics are present in non-angiosperm groups. For instance, flower structures with bisexual reproductive organs are common in the angiosperms but were also present in the extinct bennettitaleans. Fossilization of delicate and ephemeral structures such as flowers is very rare, but some Late Cretaceous fossil flowers of the saxifrage *Scandianthus* are known from Sweden. These tiny flowers (2mm long) are preserved as chemically inert charcoal.

Angiosperm leaves are fairly distinctive and different from those of the ferns, cycads and conifers. Typically, the leaves of flowering plants have a network of veins that divide and rejoin, but again such a reticulate venation also occurs in Jurassic seed-ferns and thus is not unique to angiosperms.

The critical angiosperm characteristic preservable in fossils is the enclosure of unfertilized seeds (ovules) by an outer covering or carpel. This gives a degree of protection from predators and allows fertilization to take place in a protected environment. However, fertilization may have depended upon the co-evolution of pollinating insects until the evolution of suitable stigma structures that could be fertilized by wind-carried pollen. Partial enclosure of the ovules also occurred in some Mesozoic non-angiosperm plants, such as the seed fern *Caytonia* and some cycads.

The first fossil evidence for true carpels is seen in the Early Cretaceous plant *Archaefructus* from China, but there are still some doubts as to whether this is a true angiosperm since neither the male reproductive parts nor the leaves have yet been discovered. However, there is little doubt that by the Late Jurassic or Early Cretaceous true flowering plants had evolved.

Compound leaves of a Late Eocene *Rhus*, the sumac, a tree-sized flowering plant (angiosperm) from Florissant, Colorado, USA

Grasses (Graminae, Miocene–Recent)

One of the most important evolutionary innovations in the flowering plants was that of the grasses in the Eocene or perhaps earlier. Today there are some 10,000 species of grasses, many of which have been cultivated to form our staple foods such as rice and wheat. The development of cooler and drier climates in mid-Cenozoic times has been linked to change in ocean circulation around Antarctica. This climate change also led to a reduction of global woods and forests, which in turn promoted the expansion of open savannah grasslands. This led to an expansion of grazing mammals, rodents and the like, and is perhaps connected with the development of bipedalism in our primate ancestors (*see* p.167).

Compositae (Miocene–Recent)

Another important group of flowering plants to take advantage of Cenozoic climate change were the diverse Compositae, such as the familiar weeds, sunflowers, thistles, daisies and lettuce. Typically they thrive in ground disturbed by both nature (such as after fire) and humankind (ploughed land), and today there are some 25,000 species, many of which are cultivated.

THE FOSSIL RECORD: ANIMALS WITH BACKBONES

One of the major divisions in animal life is between those animals that have a backbone (vertebral column) and are known as vertebrates and those that do not and are known as invertebrates. Possession of a backbone as part of an internal skeleton has allowed vertebrates to increase in size enormously compared with the average invertebrate. It has also provided a basic internal framework to support the body, especially on land and in the air.

As vertebrates, we humans are familiar with the important series of bones (vertebrae) that runs from the base of the skull to form a vestigial tail (coccyx) at the base of the spine. Our flexible backbone not only supports the rest of the skeleton but is an integral part of the mechanics of our movement and protects the delicate and all important spinal nerve.

All vertebrates from tiny fish to giant dinosaurs and whales have a backbone, but how did it evolve? Luckily, there are some living and extinct fossil animals that help us understand this history of development. There are primitive living fish-like animals, the lampreys, hagfish and lancelets (*Branchiostoma*), that show how the backbone developed. This anatomical evidence is supported by both the study of embryological development and the genes (the so-called homeobox genes) controlling that development. The lancelets still preserve the primitive condition in which a simple stiff but flexible rod, called the notochord, extends along the back of the animal from the tip of the head to the end of the tail. Above it lies the main nerve

Cambrian age fossils of *Haikouella*, a primitive chordate from China

cord and on either side lies a series of paired muscles whose contraction produces s-shaped sideways flexure of the body.

The fish inherited this basic body plan and style of movement, as did the earliest four-legged vertebrates – the tetrapods. It was only when the vertebrates became fully adapted for life on land that the flexure of the body changed to an up and down movement.

Those animals that have the primitive condition with a simple non-mineralized notochord are placed in the chordates along with the vertebrates. Surprisingly, there are some very ancient chordate fossils in the Cambrian deposits of the Burgess Shale of Canada (*Pikaia*) and the Chinese Chenjiang strata (*Haikouichthys* and perhaps *Myllokunmingia*).

The transformation of the notochord into a bony vertebral column initially passed through a stage where cartilage surrounded then replaced the notochord and enveloped the nerve cord and its frontal swelling – the brain. This stage is seen in the few surviving jawless (agnathan) vertebrates, the lampreys and hagfish, and in the great diversity of their fossil ancestors.

THE JAWLESS FISH (AGNATHANS)

This diverse group of strange backboned fish without jaws has a long fossil record extending from the Early Cambrian through to the present. Their heyday was in the Silurian–Devonian, when they moved from the seas into fresh waters, but they were soon in a losing battle with the jawed fish (the gnathostomes).

The mouths of the agnathans are simple openings through which water and particulate food matter is sucked. Gills are positioned in the throat region and used to sieve out food and oxygen from the water that is then flushed out through the gill openings.

Without teeth the agnathans were vulnerable to predators such as eurypterids and to the rapidly evolving jawed fish. As a result, many of the agnathans had armoured bony scales and plates for protection that made them look most un-fishlike. The downside was that the armour added weight to their bodies and restricted their movement. However, the bony plates do occur as fossils although entire animals are very rare.

A Devonian age cephalaspid jawless fish (agnathan)

JAWED FISH (GNATHOSTOMES)

Evolution of the jaws arose through modification of the skeletal supports for the foremost gills and went through several developmental stages resulting in an overall reduction in the number of gill slits. Intermediate stages are seen in extinct groups of primitive gnathostomes such as the placoderms (Silurian–Devonian) and acanthodians (Silurian–Permian). Many placoderms were armoured and some of them became very large. Fossil remains of individual plates are not uncommon in some sedimentary environments. The predatory *Dunkleosteus* of the Late Devonian grew to nearly 10m in length and had jaws lined with massive bony plates that could shear through prey.

The acanthodians (for example, *Cheiracanthus*) did not have heavy body armour and were shark-like primitive fish characterized by spines that supported the front of each fin and acted as cutwater structures and protection from predators. The spines are often the only part of the animal to be fossilized, although rare entire specimens are known.

***Cheiracanthus*, a Devonian primitive acanthodian jawed fish**

SHARKS AND RAYS

The sharks and rays are still successful groups of sea-dwelling fish, with some 800 living species, and they retain a number of primitive features. Known as chondrichthyans, they have skeletons and scales made of cartilage, which Is generally non-mineralized and does not fossilize well. Much of their fossil record is made up of teeth that have been mineralized, but in exceptional circumstances the outline of the body and some of the skeleton is preserved (for example, the Jurassic shark *Squatina* in the Solnhofen Limestone).

During the Palaeozoic the chondrichthyans were just as successful as the more advanced bony fish, and both groups suffered during the end-Permian extinction event. Although the sharks and rays gradually recovered they never diversified to the same extent as the bony fish. Nevertheless, the modern sharks still include many top predators such as the Great White shark (*Carcharodon*), although they are dwarfed by Miocene ancestors, such as *Carcharodon megalodon*, which grew to some 16m in length.

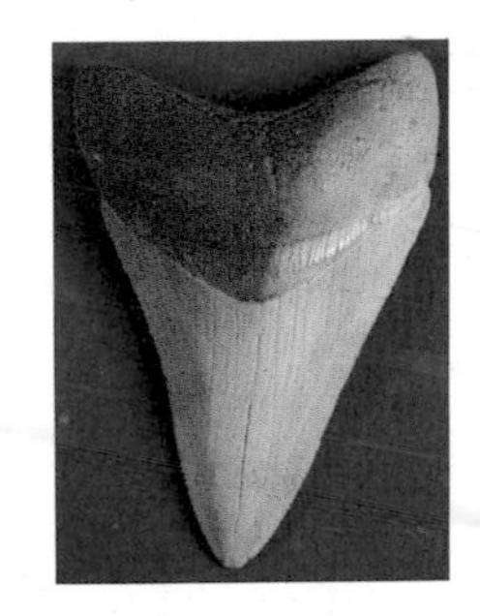

A tooth of *Carcharadon*, a Paleogene giant shark from Florida, USA

BONY FISH

With some 21,000 living species grouped into some 260 families, there is no doubt that the bony fish (the osteichthyans, Devonian–Recent) is the most diverse and successful of living vertebrate groups. This is perhaps not surprising since sea waters cover some two-thirds of the world and the bony fish have also been able to progress into freshwater rivers and lakes.

***Priscacara*, an Eocene teleost (bony fish) from Wyoming, USA**

Their history is an integral part of the evolution of the more advanced vertebrates. In Devonian times the bony fish split into two main groups, the ray-finned (actinopterygians) and the lobe-finned (sarcopterygians) fish. The former typically have fan-shaped fins with many rays and, during Palaeozoic times, were initially covered with relatively heavy bony scales, but these became reduced over time. Finally, from Late Jurassic times the modern teleost bony fish had thin body scales, reduced bony skeletons and advanced jaw structures. They underwent a dramatic diversification into a huge range of rapidly evolving forms in both marine and fresh waters.

The fossil record of the osteichthyans reflects changes in their scales and skeletons. The heavier bony scales and skeletons of Palaeozoic and Mesozoic forms tend to be well preserved and occasionally entire specimens are found (such as *Dapedium* and *Lepidotes* from the Jurassic). In contrast, the more lightly structured modern teleosts are only well preserved in exceptional circumstances, such as *Priscacara* from freshwater deposits of Wyoming in North America and the sea-dwelling *Amphiperca* from Germany.

THE LOBE-FINNED FISH

Although not very diverse, these fish are of considerable interest and importance for our understanding of one of the most critical phases in vertebrate evolution, which was the movement out of water and onto land that took place in Late Devonian times, around 370 million years ago. As their name suggests, these fish typically have two pairs of muscular lobe-shaped fins with narrow bases and relatively few bones in them, for example *Eusthenopteron*.

Survivors of this group include the lungfish (the dipnoans) and the famous 'living fossil' coelacanth (*Latimeria*). The lungfish, as the name suggests, can breathe air and for a long time were seen as transitional forms to land-living vertebrates, but we now know that the picture is more complex and interesting.

The discovery of the fossil remains of two four-legged vertebrates called *Ichthyostega* and *Acanthostega* from Devonian strata in Greenland revealed metre-long carnivorous animals with a combination of primitive and more advanced features. The presence of the legs suggested that they could walk on land but they also retained fish-like features such as long, muscular, flattened tails. New specimens of *Acanthostega* show that the ankle bones were adapted for swimming and were not powerful enough to support the animal's weight on land. Although equipped with an air-breathing lung, it also had gills.

It seems that tetrapod legs were an adaptation for living in a particular kind of watery environment. The Upper Devonian rocks in which they have been found were laid down in rivers and lakes within the huge landmass of Laurasia. From the same region, a number of other lobe-finned fish and primitive tetrapods have now been found, which close the gap between *Eusthenopteron* and *Acanthostega*.

New finds of a 370 million year old tetrapod called *Tiktaalik* from Arctic Canada reinforce the view that it was perhaps the occasional need to breathe air – between shallow water and subaerial habitats – that resulted in strengthened shoulder girdles and front (pectoral) fins. Lifting the head led to modification of the neck and the development of what is known as a 'buccal pump', in which the throat acts as a pump to gulp air and then force it into the lungs. Fossils of *Tiktaalik* preserve bones showing that it had a mobile wrist and could flex its front fins and neck. It is the oldest known animal that was capable of some movement out of the water with a seal-like motion. This lifting motion may have been the beginning of a radical shift from the sideways fish-like motion to the more up and down of later land-living tetrapods.

The environments in which they lived were also

home to the first vascular plants (*see* p.86) and many small arthropods and other invertebrates upon which these tetrapod carnivores could have fed. Being in a tropical environment, the oxygen levels in the water were often low and there would have been a decided advantage in being able to breathe air directly.

Moving onto land is not easy. Water is a supportive environment that provided protection from damaging rays and gases such as ultra-violet light and oxygen. It is no accident that we refer to a hopeless situation as being 'like a fish out of water'. The hapless fish flounders around being unable to breathe or hear, and soon its skin dries out and the fish dies of dehydration.

Any animal emerging from the water has to be pre-adapted in several ways for life in the light dry gas we know as air. It needs some means of getting about, such as legs that will support the body, waterproof skin and eye covers to prevent desiccation, lungs for breathing, ears for hearing and so on. In addition, reproduction out of water presents its own particular problems and these early tetrapods would have had to return to the water to breed. Their tadpole-like young would probably have been entirely water dwelling for some time. As we shall see, reproduction out of water requires the evolution of some protection for the embryo – a shell.

AMPHIBIAN AND REPTILE-LIKE TETRAPODS

The animals that we recognize as amphibians today (in particular, frogs and toads but also including newts and salamanders), over 4,000 species, are known as the lissamphibians. They are freshwater and terrestrial in their lifestyles and did not evolve until the Triassic. They are very different from their most ancient and extinct Late Palaeozoic ancestors which, by the Carboniferous, were already diversified into 40 families. These animals thrived in tropical swamps and were all carnivores. Many were still entirely water-dwelling fish-eaters growing to a metre or so in length, with heavy bony skulls and sharp teeth (for example, *Proterogyrinus*).

Amongst the most successful were the temnospondyls, which survived from the Carboniferous to the Triassic. They were salamander-like animals such as *Dendrerpeton* in the Carboniferous and the more massive and 2m-long crocodile-like *Eryops* of Early Permian times. The latter was largely land-living and one of the top predators of its day, feeding on small tetrapods and fish. There are many other kinds adapted to different terrestrial environments, including those with reduced limbs.

Fossil tadpole-like forms have also been found with external gills, suggesting that a true amphibian type metamorphosis was part of their reproductive cycle.

The unprotected eggs would have been laid in water where they developed into tadpole-type larvae and then adults, with the loss of the external gills.

By the Late Carboniferous and Permian, there were reptile-like tetrapods that are known as reptiliomorphs. They include *Seymouria*, an active and predatory land-living animal up to 600mm long, and the more heavily built *Diadectes*, which had short legs. One of the first land-living plant eaters, it had peg-like teeth at the front of the mouth for tearing off plant matter and broad cheek teeth for grinding it down before swallowing.

***Bradysaurus*, a Permian pareiasaur synapsid reptile from South Africa**

THE MODERN AMPHIBIANS

The 4,000 species are placed in three groups of which the first is by far the most numerous including the familiar frogs and toads (anurans), newts and salamanders (urodeles) and the strange, limbless and snake-like caecilians (gymnophiones). Most are fairly small with delicate skeletons that did not commonly fossilize except in certain special circumstances, such as fine-grained lake-bottom muds such as the Eocene deposits of Messel in Germany (for example, *Messelobatrachus*).

The anurans are very diverse and successful, having conquered a wide range of habitats even though they are dependent on water for reproduction. Their skeleton is highly adapted; the first known jumping frog (*Prosalirus*) dates from the Early Jurassic, but the oldest frogs (*Triadobatrachus*) are known from Early Triassic times and they already had a very frog-like skull.

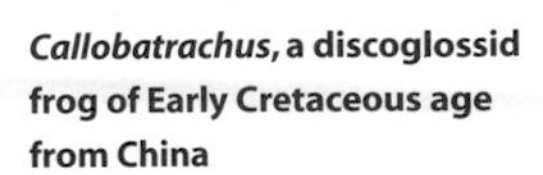

***Callobatrachus*, a discoglossid frog of Early Cretaceous age from China**

EGG-LAYING REPTILES

The ability to fertilize an egg whilst still inside its mother and then enclose the developing embryo in a membrane is a fundamental feature of a group, which includes the reptiles, birds and mammals, collectively known as amniotes. The enclosure of the embryo in a membrane and shell before birth is characteristic of the birds and reptiles. Unfortunately, eggs do not fossilize easily unless they are mineralized with calcium carbonate. The oldest fossil eggs are Triassic in age and yet there is little doubt that the first true amniote reptiles had evolved by the Middle Carboniferous, around 300 million years ago. Amazingly, the remains of two early kinds of small lizard-like reptiles were found in burned out hollow tree stumps in the

***Allaeochelys*, an Eocene turtle from Messel, Germany**

Carboniferous (coal measure) strata of Nova Scotia, Canada. *Hylonomus* and *Paleothyris* were only about 200mm long and had small, lightly built skulls and skeletons with long tails and limbs that stuck out to the side. With small sharp teeth, they fed on a diet of small insects that were abundant in these tropical forests where giant tree-sized clubmosses (lycopods, *see* p. 88) grew to 30m high.

The skulls of these earliest reptiles (anapsids) only have openings for the eyes. This is also seen in several extinct Permian and Triassic groups and in the living chelonians (such as turtles). Two other major groups based on skull form are known as the synapsids and diapsids. The synapsids have one extra skull opening and this is seen in mammals and those amniote groups from which they evolved. The diapsids have, as their name suggests two extra openings, one above the other, as is seen in the majority of living reptiles (such as the crocodiles, snakes, lizards and birds) along with the major extinct groups such as the dinosaurs and the pterosaurs. There is a fourth type, derived from the diapsids, in which the lower opening is suppressed, and this is seen in a number of extinct marine reptiles (ichthyosaurs, plesiosaurs and so on) and is called euryapsid.

The diapsids were rare during the Carboniferous, but animals such as *Petrolacosaurus* grew to 400mm long and were lizard-like carnivores with relatively long legs. In contrast, some of the Late Carboniferous synapsids, such as *Ophiacodon*, grew to 3m in length and had proportionally much larger skulls and were clearly top predators that fed on other tetrapods as well as fish and insects.

By the Permian, the supercontinent of Pangea was finally assembled with all the continents gathered together and stretching from pole to pole. Plants were gradually colonizing drier landscapes and there were major changes in vegetation and climates from the heat of equator to the glacial climates of the poles. It was within these varied landscapes and environments that the early true reptiles, with their independence of water for breeding, diversified and displaced the older tetrapod groups.

The Permian synapsids

The synapsid pelycosaurs were the most common of Early to Middle Permian reptiles and some, such as the plant-eating *Cotylorhynchus* from North America, grew up to 3m long. The similarly sized *Dimetrodon*, also from North America, was a powerful carnivore with teeth of different sizes for different functions. The large dagger-like teeth at the front corners of the mouth were for stabbing the prey and smaller curved cheek teeth cut it up in preparation for swallowing the pieces.

Like a number of pelycosaurs, *Dimetrodon* also had a series of long bony projections from its backbone (the tallest being nearly 1m long), which were covered in skin and formed a vertical sail-like structure. This is thought to have acted as a heat exchanger, allowing the cold-blooded animal to heat up quickly when turned broadside to the rising sun and perhaps as a cooler when facing the sun.

By the Late Permian, the pelycosaurs had been replaced by another synapsid group called the therapsids, many of which had powerful heavily built limbs, and included both flesh- and plant-eaters. Many were strange looking reptiles such as the plant-eating *Moschops* from South Africa, which grew to 5m

***Dimetrodon*, a Permian synapsid reptile from the USA**

in length. It had a heavily built skull that may have been used in head butting between rival males as many sheep and goats do today. The top carnivores, such as *Lycaenops*, were only about 1m long but were armed with powerful jaws and large canine teeth like a sabre-toothed cat.

Another of these Late Permian synapsid groups were the cynodonts, which diversified during the Triassic. They are of particular interest and importance because they acquired an increasing number of mammalian characters and are considered as ancestral to the mammals. For instance, *Procynosuchus* from South Africa was dog-sized and its skull was adapted for life as a predatory flesh eater with large muscles powering strong jaws and variably sized teeth for eating small tetrapods and insects.

There were several other groups of Permian reptiles, including the first marine reptiles, the mesosaurs, whose small 1m-long skeletons have been found in both South Africa and South America. They show that the two continents must have been close to one another at the time as part of the great southern supercontinent of Gondwana. There were also a number of anapsid groups including the strange plant-eating pareiasaurs such as *Scutosaurus* from Russia, which grew to 3m long with huge elephant-like legs, a deep body and a heavily boned skull covered with bony protuberances.

The diapsids produced some interesting evolutionary innovations, such as the first airborne vertebrates, the gliding weigeltisaurids such as *Coelurosauravus*. These Late Permian inhabitants of Europe and Madagascar were small lizard-like animals with greatly lengthened ribs. These were covered in skin and in gliding mode stuck out sideways to form a wing, but could be folded back against the body for normal locomotion.

THE END-PERMIAN CRASH

Permian times ended around 251 million years ago with the biggest extinction event of all time when about 90 per cent of all life in the world's oceans was wiped out. Life on land also suffered with 36 of the 48 tetrapod families and around 50 per cent of the plants becoming extinct. As yet, no single simple cause, such as a major impact event, has been identified, although it was a sudden crisis that lasted just some tens or hundreds of thousands of years. There was a vast outpouring of lavas over a huge extent of Siberia, which may have triggered changes in climate and ocean chemistry. The ultimate cause is still unknown but its devastating effects are all too clear and Earth was left in a desolate state.

THE REPTILES OF THE TRIASSIC

Following the end-Permian extinction event there were important changes in the evolution of the vertebrates. Some Permian amniotes, such as the synapsid dicynodonts and cynodonts, made a significant recovery and, as we shall see, were particularly important in mammalian evolution. However, a major new group of diapsid reptiles, known as the archosaurs, also appeared. They gave rise to the dinosaurs, birds, pterosaurs and crocodiles as well as some smaller extinct groups. The other important Triassic groups of diapsids were marine reptiles such as the ichthyosaurs, plesiosaurs, placodonts and nothosaurs.

To begin with, the Triassic world was similar to that of the Late Permian, with the supercontinent of Pangea stretching from pole to pole. Within this huge landmass some groups of vertebrates such as the dicynodonts were able to disperse worldwide. The fossil remains of dicynodonts

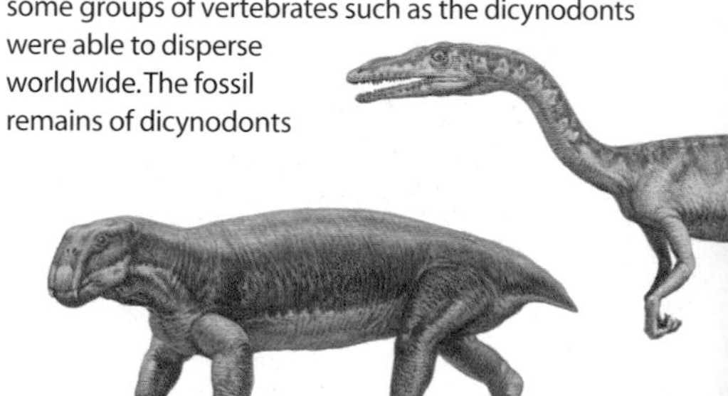

such as *Lystrosaurus* are now found widely distributed on separate continents. Many Early Triassic fossil sites show a progressive increase in desert-like dry subtropical conditions through the period. This is partly a result of a northward movement of the whole supercontinent but also may reflect a more general global increase in dry climates. As a result there were significant changes in the plants, with conifers becoming increasingly common by the Late Triassic.

Triassic reptiles included (from left to right) the dicynodont *Lystrosaurus*, the predatory dinosaur *Coelophysis* and the herbivorous dinosaur *Plateosaurus*

The archosaurs

One of the earliest archosaurs was a 1.5m-long crocodile-like carnivore with short legs, called *Proterosuchus*. It lived in South Africa from latest Permian times and preyed upon the dicynodonts and other small reptiles. The first wave of diversity in the archosaurs happened in the Middle Triassic. Archosaurs, such as *Euparkeria*, also from South Africa, that were no more than 50cm long, could probably run on their two hind legs and walk on all fours. They were all flesh eaters with the smaller ones feeding mostly on insects and other small animals.

A crocodile, a surviving saurischian archosaur

Dinosauromorphs

Another main development of the archosaurs in the Middle to Late Triassic was the appearance of dinosaur-like reptiles such as *Marasuchus* in South America. This lightly built and fast-moving carnivore grew to some 1.2m long and probably hunted small cynodonts and any other small creatures it could catch. It was another of the first upright-standing (bipedal) reptiles and had hind legs that were twice as long as its forearms. The

***Euparkia*, an Early Triassic archosaur**

body, arms, s-shaped neck and head were counter-balanced by a long tail. *Marasuchus* and its relative *Lagosuchus*, also from South America, are dinosaur-like in the structure of their legs and hips and consequently are called dinosauromorphs. These are the most likely ancestors of the dinosaurs, although surprisingly the dinosaurs' closest relatives seem to be the pterosaurs.

Pterosaurs

Another group of archosaurs was the first of the vertebrates to take up powered flight, the pterosaurs. This was a very successful group, which lived for around 150 million years alongside the dinosaurs from the Late Triassic to the end of the Cretaceous. It included the largest flying animals ever to have existed, the gigantic *Quetzalcoatlus* of latest Cretaceous times in Texas, USA. It had a wingspan of up to 12m and was the size of a small plane. All the pterosaurs had short bodies, long necks, large heads and folding wings, made of a thin skin membrane reinforced with hair-like fibres, which was stretched between highly modified and elongate fingers and the body. Inevitably, for a flying animal the skeleton had hollow bones to reduce weight.

One of the earliest pterosaurs was *Eudimorphodon* from Europe. Its lightly built skeleton included a large but lightly framed skull with specialized teeth for catching fish, and a long thin tail. The hands had a highly elongate fourth finger, which supported a wing membrane of skin with a span of up to 1 m. This was already a well adapted and specialized flying reptile, showing that the origin of the pterosaurs probably dates back to the Middle Triassic.

Without the agility and tough feathered wings of the birds, the pterosaurs were restricted in their habitats and way of life. For taking off they probably depended upon headwinds and were generally vulnerable to any fast-moving predator on

***Sinopterus*, an Early Cretaceous pterosaur from China**

the ground. Consequently, they tended to inhabit inaccessible windy places where rising thermals or updrafts were common, such as rocky cliffs, especially close to the sea or other waters well stocked with fish.

The crocodiles

The surviving eight genera of crocodiles (including alligators and gavials) still thrive in both fresh and marine tropical waters around the world. They are the descendants of a much larger and very ancient group of archosaurs that stretch back to the Late Triassic. And, unlike so many other archosaur groups, the crocodiles (or crocodilians as we should call this large group) survived the end-Cretaceous extinction event.

Curiously, for a group that typically has long skulls, bodies and tails and walked on all fours, it is thought that the crocodilians originated from Late Triassic reptiles that mostly walked on two hind legs (bipedal) and ate small insects. Animals such as *Ornithosuchus* had long muscular tails and quite slender bodies held on long hind legs, and smaller arms that could nevertheless occasionally be used for walking on all fours. Known as ornithosuchids, phytosaurs, aetosaurs and rauisuchians, this group included some very large animals and the specialized structure of their ankles links them with the later crocodilians.

The Late Triassic aetosaurs, such as the 3m-long *Stagonolepis* from Scotland, were the first plant-

A well preserved Neogene age crocodile skull from Abu Dhabi

eating archosaurs with pointed shovel-like snouts and small peg-shaped teeth. They had an extensive body armour of bony plates to protect them from large rauisuchian predators. *Saurosuchus* was a Late Triassic rauisuchian flesh eater from South America that grew up to 7m long. Although somewhat crocodile-like, it walked on all four of its relatively long legs, which were tucked in under its body. This gave a much more efficient, and more mammal-like, way of running with an up and down movement of the backbone rather the side to side flexure seen in many reptiles and the modern crocodiles. The backbone of *Saurosuchus* sags down between the skull and shoulder, arches up over to the hips and then sags down into the tail, only to rise again at its tip.

REPTILES TAKE TO THE SEAS

Triassic times also saw diapsid reptile groups take to the seas, but we know little about their evolutionary origins. Animals such as *Pachypleurosaurus* from the Middle Triassic marine strata of Europe grew to 1m long and had elongate bodies with long tails, necks and small heads. They swam in a fish-like way using sinuous sideways beating of their deep tails and small paddle-like limbs that were probably used for steering.

The placodonts were another short-lived group of Triassic marine reptiles with relatively unmodified legs. *Placodus* is an example that superficially looks like a heavily built land-living reptile. However, the loose articulation of the limbs with the body show that they were not used for walking on land. The teeth are modified for eating shellfish. The spoon-shaped front teeth stick out and were used for grabbing shellfish from the seabed. Heavy flat cheek teeth

***Stenopterygius*, a Jurassic ichthyosaur from Holzmaden, Germany**

covered the floor and roof of the mouth and were used to crush the shells so that the meat could be extracted and swallowed.

The ichthyosaurs (meaning 'fish lizards') were the one group of Triassic sea-dwelling reptiles that continued to become more diverse and numerous beyond the end of the period (for example, *Ichthyosaurus*) and into the Cretaceous, only to die away again in the Late Cretaceous. They were active predators with streamlined, dolphin-shaped bodies for fast pursuit of their fish and squid-like belemnite (*see* p.62) prey. Their limbs were modified into seal-like paddles for steering and they had powerful fish-like tails. The jaws were prolonged into beak-like structures full of sharp conical teeth and the eyes were often unusually large, suggesting that they depended upon sight for hunting their prey in gloomy and perhaps deep waters. Some Late Triassic ichthyosaurs, such as *Cymbospondylus*, were the largest, growing to lengths of up to 10m.

Even larger were some of the plesiosaurs, such as *Liopleurodon*. It had a large head with powerful jaws and broad-based sharp teeth. The other group of the plesiosaurs consists of the long-necked plesiosauroids such as the 5m-long Late Jurassic *Muraenosaurus*. As a group the plesiosauroids had relatively small heads but large powerful and highly adapted, paddle-like, limbs for underwater swimming.

The lepidosaurs include 4,470 species of living lizards and 2,920 species of snakes as well as the lizard-like tuatara (*Sphenodon*) from New Zealand. The latter can be considered as a 'living fossil', since its sphenodont ancestors were the first recognizable lepidosaurs in Late Triassic times. The true lizards and snakes are grouped as the squamates with six branches (clades), including the iguanas, geckos, skinks, ambisphaenids, anguimorphs and snakes, all characterized by their flexible skulls.

Their fossil record is patchy and their interrelationships not yet clear. The anguimorphs are the most diverse, including the monitor lizards such as the extinct 7m-long giant goanna (*Megalania*) of the Pleistocene in Australia. Three families became adapted to life in Late Cretaceous seas. Of these the mosasaurs were ferocious predators with jaws that were up to a metre long and armed with sharp conical teeth. Some of them were ocean going and widely distributed, such as the 11m-long *Tylosaurus*.

The origin of the limbless snakes with backbones of up to 500 vertebrae is problematic. However, the discovery of a primitive 93-million-year-old Late Cretaceous snake which retains its hind limbs suggests that they may have originated from terrestrial burrowing reptiles rather than marine ones.

BIRDS

Today, there are over 9,000 species of birds, considerably more than mammal species, and these birds are classified into some 153 families. They have a fossil record stretching back to the Late Jurassic, when the earliest birds lived alongside the dinosaurs and competed with the flying pterosaur reptiles for air-space. There are another 77 extinct bird families which only have fossil representation, showing that there has been much evolutionary change and turnover within the group over the last 140 million years. At the height of their diversity in the Pleistocene, there may have been as many as 20,000 living bird species. Although birds today seem quite distinct from other groups of vertebrates, their fossil record shows that to begin with the distinction between birds and some dinosaurs was distinctly blurred.

Today, birds range in size from the miniscule hummingbirds to the flightless ostrich. Previously, there were some significantly larger flightless birds such as *Aepyornis*, the so-called 'elephant bird' of Madagascar, which grew to 3.7m high, but Stirton's Mihirung (*Dromornis*) from Australia was probably the heaviest bird ever, weighing up to 500kg.

The great adaptive advantage of the warm-blooded birds over most reptiles is their covering of feathers, which insulates and protects the body and provides a repairable cover for the wings as well as camouflage and display functions. The birds are as successful in occupying a vast range of habitats as any other vertebrate group, including the mammals. They can live in polar regions (for example, Emperor penguins in Antarctica), migrate thousands of kilometres annually (as do swallows, for example), fly over high mountains, and some can live on water. The secret of their success has been their adaptability, mobility, acute sensory apparatus and intelligence. Some birds, such as Caledonian crows, can learn to make and use tools. The main constraint on their way of life is the need to lay their eggs somewhere that is as safe as possible from predators.

***Cathayornis*, an Early Cretaceous enantiornithine bird from China**

THE FOSSIL RECORD OF BIRDS

The oldest known fossil bird is the Late Jurassic *Archaeopteryx*, one of the most famous fossils known. It was first discovered in 1861 by quarrymen working the lithographic limestones of Solnhofen in Bavaria, and bought by the English anatomist Richard Owen for the British Museum.

In 1864 Owen described *Archaeopteryx* as a rook-sized bird with 'feathered instruments of flight. He also pointed out some reptilian features such as a long straight bony tail and teeth in its beak-like jaws. But it was Thomas Henry Huxley who realized that it was one of the first fossils to clearly demonstrate an evolutionary missing link between two classes of organisms and thus provide strong palaeontological support for Charles Darwin's recently formulated theory of evolution. At that time the possession of feathers was thought to be a unique bird (avian) character. Several specimens of *Archaeopteryx* have now been found, and some experts claim that it can be linked with some small bipedal dinosaurs.

Recent fossil discoveries of feathered dinosaurs, especially in China, have shown that feathers are not uniquely avian. Furthermore, the dinosaur–bird evolution has been greatly strengthened by the realization that a number of small, lightly built and bipedal groups of theropod dinosaurs, such as the dromaeosaurs and troodontids, have distinctly bird-like characters. So much so that they are called the paravians by some experts.

In general the fossil record of birds is not as good as that of the mammals because of their mode of life and lack of teeth. However, recent studies have been able to target a number of fossil sites that do preserve bird remains, such as the deposits of lakes, lagoons, caves and limestone fissures. The Solnhofen deposits are lagoonal whilst many of the Chinese and Spanish localities are lake deposits, as are the Eocene deposits of Messel in Germany (*see* p.5). Until the discovery of the Early Cretaceous bird fossils of China and Spain, there was a significant gap in their fossil record between the 150-million-year-old *Archaeopteryx* and the Late Cretaceous and Cenozoic fossil birds.

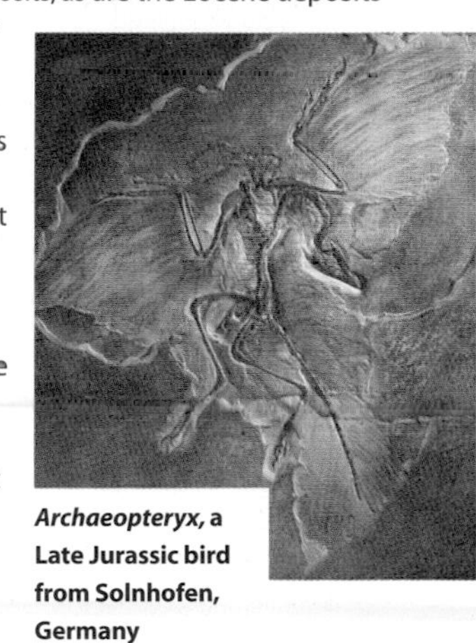

***Archaeopteryx*, a Late Jurassic bird from Solnhofen, Germany**

Now we know that this interval saw the radiation of some birdlike groups such as the

Alvarezsauridae, whose relationships to the birds have now been confirmed. In addition there were several unique and more birdlike groups such as the Enantiornithes, Hesperornithiformes and Ichthyornithiformes, all of which were extinct by the end of the Cretaceous.

Reconstruction of *Archaeopteryx* with its long dinosaur-like bony tail

The 'opposite birds' – the Enantiornithes (Cretaceous)

This major group of Cretaceous and globally distributed birds lived alongside the dinosaurs and early mammals. They are characterized by the structure of their limb bones and are known as the 'opposite birds'. This is because their shoulder girdle and feet developed with a different structural pattern from other birds, including all living birds, which are collectively known as the Ornithurae.

Most were small sparrow-sized, toothed birds and strong flyers such as *Sinornis* from China. But by the end of the Cretaceous there were some turkey-sized forms with wingspans of a metre or so (for example, *Enantiornis*) and there was a flightless lineage of fast runners.

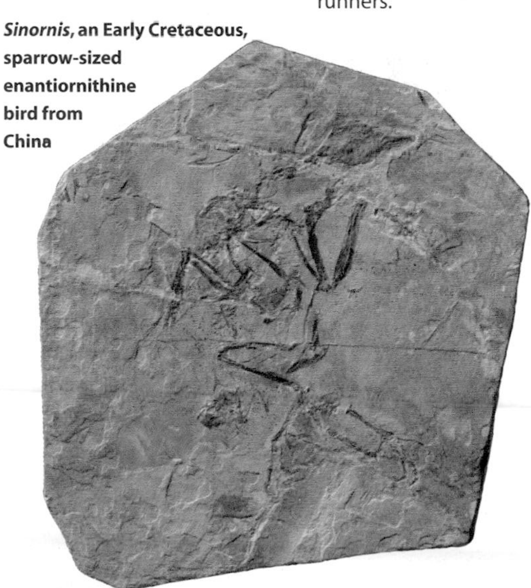

***Sinornis*, an Early Cretaceous, sparrow-sized enantiornithine bird from China**

Hesperornithiformes (Early–Late Cretaceous)

This group of toothed birds had very reduced wings and they are generally considered as flightless diving birds that evolved from flying ancestors. Their long toes may have ended in lobes or been connected by a web of skin, thus making their feet effective for propulsion through their watery habitats. Remains of the metre-long *Hesperornis* have been found in the Late Cretaceous Niobrara Chalk from Kansas, USA, which was deposited in a shallow warm sea in which the birds hunted fish.

Ichthyornithiformes (Early–Late Cretaceous)

Another group of toothed birds known from the Niobrara Chalk, but these were gull-sized fliers with fully developed wings and deeply keeled bony sternum (for example, *Ichthyornis*) as seen in modern birds. They had a relatively large head with large toothed jaws and the bony tail was reduced to a short pygostyle, close to the condition seen in modern birds. They probably represent a long extinct early radiation of ornithurine carinate birds.

The Hesperornithiformes and Ichthyornithiformes are also grouped as carinates, since they have a deepened keel (sternum) to which enlarged flight muscles are attached.

CENOZOIC 'MODERN' BIRDS

The palaeognaths (Palaeocene–Recent)

This is essentially a Gondwanan group of birds today, both flying and flightless, known mainly from South America, Africa and Australia, such as the flightless ratites (for example the rheas). Their fossil record is poor in the early Cenozoic with most groups being no older than Oligocene in age, but there is some evidence for their earlier occurrence. It is within this group that the biggest living and fossil birds are found. Today, the Ostrich is the largest bird, weighing up to 160kg and standing up to 2.8m tall, but some fossil species were much larger (such as *Aepyornis*, *see* above).

Evidence for their earlier occurrence comes from fossils that date from the Palaeocene and Eocene (for example, *Lithornis* from Wyoming, USA) and their locations suggest that the group may have originated in the Northern hemisphere, but there is no general consensus about their origins. Overall, the group retains some primitive theropod and avian characters, especially in the form of the palate.

The neognaths

The wonderful diversity of modern birds, from ducks and chickens through cranes, storks, owls and swifts to the songbirds, has resulted in the living species arranged into some 140 families. They include the falconiformes (falcons, eagles and vultures), amongst which are the largest living flying birds, the condors with a wingspan of 3m. However, their fossil relatives, the teratorns, were even bigger, with the Late Miocene *Argentavis* having a truly spectacular wingspan of 7.5m and a 55cm-long skull.

Most neognaths have evolved over the last 55 million years since Eocene times, except for the songbirds, the passeriforms. These comprise 60 per cent of all living birds with some 5,700 species, whose amazing diversification has occurred over the last 20 million years since the Early Miocene. However, their origin also dates back to Early Cenozoic times. The passeriforms are perching birds that have specialized feet with a posterior toe for grasping branches.

Overall, the evolution of the birds shows a significant extinction of the Mesozoic forms at the end of the Cretaceous followed by two phases of diversification. The evolution and radiation of the Early Cenozoic groups parallels that of the mammals with what is called an evolutionary bottleneck at the end of the Cretaceous. It is assumed that all Cenozoic birds must have evolved from a few survivors of the end-Cretaceous extinction event. There was an initial burst in diversity at the beginning of the Cenozoic followed by a further dramatic increase in the song-birds in the Miocene.

MAMMALS

Mammals form a distinct group of some 5,400 species, characterized by being warm blooded, having hair instead of scales, and giving birth to live young (except the monotremes, *see* below), suckled with milk from mammary glands on the mother. Typically, the young are cared for over an extended period but this varies enormously. Living mammals have a single (dentary) bone in the jaw instead of the four bones seen in the cynodont jaw, and that jawbone now articulates via a single joint with the skull. One of the 'missing' bones (the articular) forms one of the tiny bone elements (the malleus) of the middle ear in the mammals. They produce a sophisticated organ of balance and hearing that can detect high frequency sounds, such as squeaks and buzzes, transmitted through air. This apparatus was particularly useful for small primitive mammals, many of which were active, likely nocturnal and tree-dwelling animals that fed on insects.

Mammalian teeth are complex in form and those of the upper jaw meet those of the lower jaw precisely to chew food before digestion. Rapid conversion of food to energy promotes the high metabolic rates necessary to maintain an active warm-blooded existence. Mammalian teeth are not replaced continuously but typically a juvenile 'milk set' is replaced although some other cheek teeth only form once.

The mammalian brain is relatively large and the lobes of the forebrain, connected to highly developed senses, are greatly enlarged. They enclose the more primitive elements of the reptile brain and a novel brain structure found only in the mammals, the neocortex.

There are over 20 major groups of living mammals, most of which have evolved within the Cenozoic, and another eight or nine groups that became extinct in the Cenozoic. Two of the living mammal groups have long evolutionary histories stretching back into the Mesozoic, and show distinctly primitive characters – the pouch-bearing marsupials (Middle Cretaceous–Recent) and the egg-laying monotremes (Early Cretaceous–Recent). Modern placental mammals, with prolonged gestation in a uterus, and the marsupials, in which immature young are retained in a pouch, are traditionally grouped together as the therians and separated from the more primitive monotremes.

Mammalian features of soft-tissue anatomy are rarely preserved in the fossil record. Only those features present in bones, such as jaw structure and teeth, can be used to detail the evolution of mammals. Their fossil record reveals a complex history involving many extinct groups.

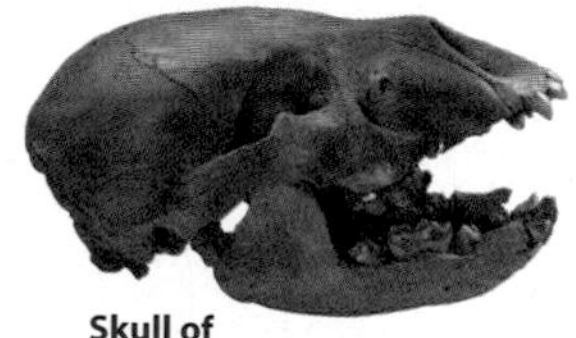

Skull of an ice age cave bear

There are half a dozen or so extinct mammal groups that are mostly known from the Mesozoic, some of which extend back into Late Triassic times. At that time, the boundary between mammals and reptiles was far less clear than it is today, and indeed the separation is somewhat arbitrary. Nevertheless, there have been significant evolutionary changes and developments over this extended period.

Towards the mammals

The mammals originated in Late Triassic times from the cynodonts, whose evolutionary history extends back into the Late Permian. The cynodonts ranged in size from weasel- to dog-sized animals, initially with a sprawling form as seen in reptiles. However, even the earliest fossil cynodonts, such as *Procynosuchus*, show mammal-like features in the lower jaw and palate.

There was significant turnover and origination within the cynodonts throughout the Triassic, and these show developmental steps towards a more mammal-like condition. One of the major changes was that of posture, wlth the legs being brought in under the body instead of sprawling out to the side in the more typical reptilian posture. This brought changes in the limb joints and musculature and the flexure of the backbone from sideways to up and down.

By the Late Triassic there were groups of cynodonts such as the tritylodonts, for example *Kayentatherium* from North America, that were distinctly mammal-like but still lacked the true mammal jaw articulation. They were plant eaters with rodent-like skulls and large, specialized cheek teeth for grinding plant food.

The first mammals

The oldest mammal fossils of Late Triassic age, such as *Adelobasileus* from Texas, USA, are rare and fragmentary but include a partial braincase with some mammalian features. Younger specimens, such as the Early Jurassic *Sinoconodon* from China, are better preserved and show true mammalian articulation of the jaw but also retain some primitive cynodont features in their teeth.

The best known true mammals are the Early Jurassic morganucodonts (Late Triassic–Late Jurassic), from England and *Megazostrodon* from South Africa, for which a complete skeleton is known. This small, 10cm-long, shrew-like animal, which only weighed about 25g, retained some cynodont-like features in the forelimbs. Nevertheless, it was active and probably nocturnal with mammalian-style teeth.

The skull of an oreodontid mammal of Pliocene age from South Dakota, USA

Mesozoic mammals

Recent decades have seen the discovery of increasing numbers of primitive mammal fossils, especially teeth and jaw fragments but also very occasionally more complete skeletal remains. These animals include the Early Jurassic kuenotheriids (for example, *Kuenotherium* from South Wales, UK) and, by the Late Jurassic, eight other groups such as the docodonts, triconodonts (Early Jurassic–Cretaceous), symmetrodonts (Late Jurassic–Cretaceous) and multituberculates (Late Jurassic–Oligocene). Their classification is particularly based on dental characters and their diversity tells us that there was a much more extensive Mesozoic radiation of mammals around the world than previously thought.

Jeholodens was a mouse-sized (20cm) triconodont insect-eater that lived in China in the Early Cretaceous, and is known from a beautifully preserved skeleton. It retained primitive sprawling hind limbs but more advanced forelimbs and was probably ground-living. Another recent amazing triconodont from the same deposits is *Repenomamus giganticus*. At some 14kg in weight, this was the size of the present-day Virginia opossum and was the largest known early mammal. The remains of a baby ceratopsian dinosaur (*Psittacosaurus*) were found in its stomach, suggesting that *Repenomamus* was an active predator.

Repenomamus* with a baby *Psittacosaurus

A complete Early Cretaceous symmetrodont, *Zhangheotherium*, is also known from China. Again, this was a small mouse-sized, insect-eating animal with sprawling limbs but a more flexible and advanced shoulder articulation. Although its ear structure is also quite primitive, it is thought that the symmetrodonts were closer to the therian mammals than the multi-tuberculates, which were a longer surviving group.

The multituberculates were abundant and diverse small mammals that ranged from mouse- to rabbit-sized, with superficially rodent-like teeth. Different genera were adapted to different modes of life and some were clearly tree dwellers. Complete specimens of *Kryptobataar* from the Late Cretaceous of Mongolia had a very narrow and rigid pelvis with a birth canal only 3–4mm wide, showing that it probably gave birth to very immature live young. *Ptilodus* from the Palaeocene of Canada had a prehensile tail and could rotate its feet backwards for descending trees face first. The multituberculates survived the end-Cretaceous extinction event but were eventually displaced by the real rodents.

As we all know, modern (placental) mammals bear live young but the more primitive monotremes still retain the reptilian habit of laying eggs. It is not known whether these early mammals bore live young or eggs, but the extremely small size of the pelvic opening suggests that they are more likely to have given birth to live but very immature young. This is similar to the marsupial condition and requires prolonged maternal feeding and care in a pouch.

Monotremes

Modern egg-laying monotremes, such as the duck-billed platypus and the spiny echidnas, have an Australasian distribution. Of the living monotremes only the juvenile platypus has teeth and these are unerupted cheek teeth in juveniles. Considering they are very primitive mammals, their fossil record is curiously restricted and until recently only extended back to the Middle Miocene around 15 million years ago in Australia. However, the discovery of fossil platypus-like teeth from the Palaeocene of Argentina suggests that they are a more ancient Gondwanan group. These have now been linked with older Cretaceous and Jurassic fossils from Australia and Madagascar and called the australosphenids.

Marsupials

As we have seen, it is likely that some early primitive mammal groups were marsupial, but the first fossils that are generally accepted as marsupials come from North America, such as *Alphadon* of Late Cretaceous age. Like living marsupials it has three premolars and four molars, compared with four or five premolars and three molars in placental mammals.

Marsupials had a much greater distribution in the past than today. They probably spread in Early Cretaceous times with one branch extending from North America through South America into Antarctica and Australia. Then, in the Early Cenozoic,

***Palaeochiropteryx*, a fossil Eocene bat from Messel, Germany**

another branch extended from North America into Eurasia and Africa where they survived until the Miocene before being replaced by placental mammals. Marsupials were also replaced in North America during the Miocene by Asian placentals but were later partly replenished from South America.

Australian marsupials were protected by the isolation of the continent following the break up of Gondwanaland. They diversified into many groups that show convergent evolution with the placentals. For example, the recently extinct *Thylacinus* was a marsupial wolf-like animal and the Pleistocene plant-eater *Diprotodon* was hippo-sized. Four main living groups are recognized: the dasyuromorphs, such as the Tasmanian Devil; the peramelemorphs, such as bandicoots; the notoryctemorphs such as the marsupial moles; and the diprotodonts, for example the extinct *Diprotodon* and 143 living species including kangaroos, possums, koalas and wombats.

South American marsupials also flourished until the Late Cenozoic when the continent was reconnected to North America. Again there was convergent evolution, with a dominance of insectivores and carnivores (15 extinct families) including marsupial shrews, dogs, cats (for example the Pliocene *Thylacosmilus*) and bears. These South American marsupials lived alongside some unique and very strange placental mammals (*see* below).

PLACENTAL (EUTHERIAN) MAMMALS

The 5,000 and more species of living placental mammals show a remarkable diversity into some 20 major groups and there are another six or so extinct fossil groups. Living mammals range from the primitive armadillos, sloths and ant-eaters (xenarthrans) to the elephants (proboscideans), whales (cetaceans), bats (chiropterans) and humans (primates). The extinct fossil groups, such as mesonychids and creodonts, are much less familiar except to experts and fossil enthusiasts.

Although most of these groups have reasonable fossil records there are some that are poorly represented and whose origins have been highly problematic. The recent molecular comparisons of living mammals and their cladistic analysis initially created a new set of problems, but the main patterns have become clearer in the last decade or so. But since molecular data cannot be retrieved from the extinct mammal groups, their inter-relationships within the scheme often remain problematic.

According to molecular clock estimates, the divergence of the marsupials from the more advanced placentals (eutherians) happened between 130–185 million years ago. The earliest fossil eutherian known is the 125 million-year-old *Eomaia* from the Early Cretaceous of China, which was yet again shrew-sized (16cm long) and only weighed about 20g. It had long fingers and toes with curved claws that were probably an adaptation for active climbing. The beautiful Chinese fossil even preserves the remains of its fur coat.

Afrotherians

In the overall evolution (phylogeny) of mammal groups, the first main branch was the afrotherians, which diverged in the Late Cretaceous just over 100 million years ago, according to molecular clock estimates. As their name suggests, they include groups of African placentals such as aardvarks (tubulidentates), tenrecs (tenrecomorphs), golden moles (chrysochlorids) and elephant shrews (macroscelideans). Another branch of afrotherians is the paenungulates and includes the elephants (proboscideans), sea-cows (sirenians) and hyraxes (hyracoids).

Of these, the proboscideans have the best fossil record, which stretches back into the Early Eocene, with animals like the North African *Moeritherium*, which was a 1m-long hippo-like beast. From these small beginnings evolved one of the most successful groups of large mammals, which eventually were distributed across Africa, Eurasia and the Americas. It included the extinct gomphotheres, stegodontids, mastodonts, mammutids and the surviving elephants.

Xenarthrans

The xenarthrans include the armadillos, sloths and ant-eaters. Generally the teeth are much reduced and the group includes some unique large animals of South America, such as the extinct giant armoured armadillos, for example *Glyptodon*, which weighed 2 tonnes, and ground sloths such as the 6m-long *Megatherium*. The ground sloths ranged widely into North America and only died out around 11,000 years ago.

Laurasiatherians

The laurasiatherians include the insectivores, such as the hedgehogs, moles and shrews (lipotyphlans) and bats (chiroptera), as basal members of a clade called the ferungulates. These basal laurasiatherians have fossil records extending back to the Early Cenozoic; for example, *Archaeonycteris* was an Eocene bat and *Pholidocerus* a dog-sized hedgehog, both known from Messel (*see* p.5).

The more advanced members of the ferungulate clade form a large group that includes the cetartiodactyls (pigs, cattle and whales), perissodactyls (horses, tapirs and rhinoceroses), carnivores (cats, dogs, weasels, bears and seals) and pholidotans (pangolins).

The cetartiodactyls include even-toed ungulates (artiodactyls) such as the pigs and hippos (suiforms) and cattle, deer, giraffes, camels and antelopes (selenodontids). They all seem to have originated from small rabbit-sized plant-eating animals such as *Diacodexis* from the Eocene of North America. Surprisingly, molecular analysis shows that the whales also belong in this group. But there is Eocene age fossil evidence (*Pakicetus*) from Pakistan that the whales have indeed all descended from a land-living artiodactyl.

The perissodactyls are distinguished by having odd numbers of toes and they diversified in Eocene times to become the dominant browsing plant-eaters. Fossil remains of the largest land mammal of all time, belonging to a perissodactyl called *Paraceratherium*, have been found in Pakistan. This was a giant Oligocene rhinoceros that stood 5.4m high at the shoulder and weighed more than 15 tonnes. By contrast, horses evolved from small dog-sized animals such as the Eocene age *Hyracotherium*, whose fossil remains have been found in North America. It had four hoofed toes on each front leg and three hoofed toes on each back. Initially woodland browsers, the horses adapted to become larger grazers of the newly evolving grasses in the Oligocene when cooling climates reduced woodlands and forests. Their legs became longer and the number of toes progressively reduced until finally the Pliocene horse *Pliohippus* and its living descendants have a single and central weight-bearing toe with two adjacent toes reduced to bony splints.

Two important extinct groups of perissodactyls were the brontotheres and chalicotheres, which have relatively good fossil records in North America and Asia. The brontotheres were heavily built rhino-like browsing mammals such as the Late Eocene *Brontops* from North America, which stood 2.5m high at the shoulder and had a prominent nose horn. Of similar height, the chalicotheres were very strange animals with horse-like heads, short back legs and disproportionately long forelimbs, each with three fingers ending in hooves. They probably could rise on their strong back legs and used their long arms to pull down high branches with tender shoots. When they walked they adopted an ape-like form of knuckle walking.

The carnivorans and pholidotans

Meat-eating cats, dogs, hyenas, weasels and seals (carnivorans) are characterized by a pair of enlarged teeth on each side of the jaws, known as carnassial teeth, which interact as powerful shears for cutting flesh and even, in the hyenas, for breaking bones. The canine teeth are also often enlarged into dagger-like teeth for puncturing skin to hold and kill prey. These teeth reached maximum size in the sabre-toothed cats such as the Pleistocene *Smilodon* from North America. The evolutionary origins of this group are not yet clear but there are related fossils from the Early Cenozoic such as *Vulpavus* and the Eocene dog *Hesperocyon*.

The seals, walrus and sea lions form an aquatic group of carnivorans (the pinnipeds) and they probably arose from land-living bear-like ancestors such as the Late Oligocene *Enaliarctos* from North America.

The toothless ant-eating pangolins are very strange scaly-skinned mammals that used to be placed with the xenarthran anteaters and armadillos. Molecular data has resulted in their transfer to a relationship with the carnivorans.Today, seven species of pangolin are scattered across Africa and Southeast Asia, but they have a more widely distributed fossil record from North America and Europe.The earliest pangolin is the Eocene *Eomanis* from Messel in Germany.

Skull of the ice age sabretooth cat *Smilodon* from North America

THE EUARCHONTOGLIRES

Two major groups comprise the euarchontoglires: archontans such as the primates, tree shrews (scandentians) and flying lemurs (dermopterans), and glires such as the rodents (rodentia), rabbits (lagomorphs) and the like. Basal archontans are represented by the plesiadapiforms that radiated in the Early Cenozoic through North America and western Europe. *Plesiadapis* is a well known squirrel-like animal, 80cm long and weighing up to 5kg. It had strong claws for climbing and highly derived rodent-like teeth for grinding plant food.

Of the rodents, rabbits and their relatives, the former have been a phenomenal evolutionary success, making up some 40 per cent of all mammal species (2,000 living species). The anatomical reason for their success has been their continuously growing curved incisor teeth which are self sharpening and can gnaw through hard plant material like wood.

Because of their abundance, rodents have a good fossil record, although it mostly consists of teeth and jaw fragments. More complete skeletons are known from Early Cenozoic times such as *Paramys* from North America and Eurasia. There was even a Miocene rodent from Venezuela called *Phoberomys*, which was 3m long, stood 1.3m at the shoulder and weighed 700kg. It was probably semi-aquatic like the present-day capybara.

THE EXTINCTION OF THE PLEISTOCENE MEGAFAUNA

Many of the largest mammals evolved over the last 5 million years, during an interval of repeated glaciations in the northern hemisphere and marked climate changes in the tropics and southern hemisphere. The Americas, Eurasia and Australia all had mammal faunas with many species more than 40 kg in weight, but over 70 per cent of these became extinct within the last few tens of thousands of years of the Pleistocene. The giants were mostly gone by the beginning of Holocene time around 11,000 years ago. Africa is the only major continent whose megafauna (elephants, rhinoceros, giraffe) has survived through this interval, though it may not last much longer. There are several hypotheses for the cause of the extinctions:

1. Climate changes affected vegetation and other critical resources so severely that the large herbivores could not adapt;
2. Hunting of megafauna ('overkill') by early *Homo sapiens*, as they increased their geographic range and skill as hunters;
3. Normal cycles of high and low abundance reduced megafaunal species to fatally low population levels;
4. Cascade effects from species to species, for example predators became extinct after their prey disappeared;
5. A combination of any or all of these processes.

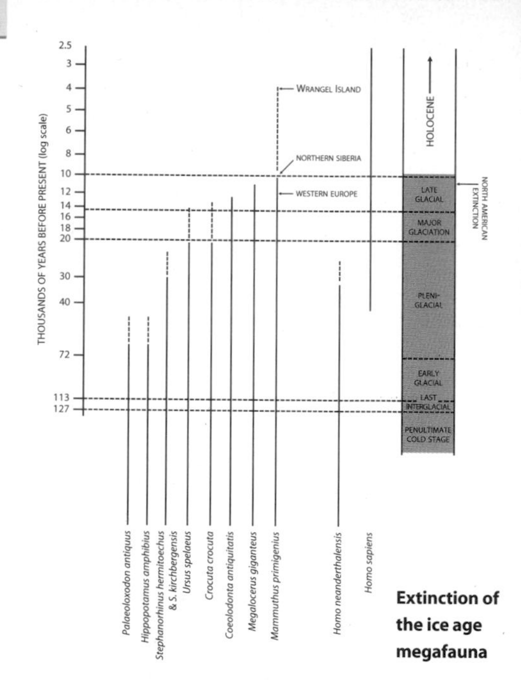

Extinction of the ice age megafauna

There is no doubt that climate change impacted life on all continents during the late Pleistocene. Vegetation distributions changed dramatically as global climates swung back and forth between cold, dry glacials and warm, wet interglacials. Animals such as elephants, hippos, big cats, and giant deer lived in England during these warm phases but were replaced by hairy mammoths, woolly rhinoceros, bison and reindeer during the colder phases. These cycles went on for hundreds of thousands of years, but then nearly all of these animals became extinct at the end of the last ice age, around 11,000 years ago.

Data on the pace of change and extinction around the world have been compared with the timing of colonization of different continents by Palaeolithic human hunters. The 'overkill' hypothesis argues that even a small population of mobile human hunters could have disrupted large mammal populations. The timing of modern human immigrations to Eurasia, North America and Australia are similar to the timing of megafaunal extinctions on these continents, providing strong evidence that human hunting was a factor in the extinctions. In Australia, where climate change was not as extreme as in the glaciated areas of the northern latitudes, 55 species of large mammals, birds, and reptiles went extinct soon after the arrival of the ancestors of the Aborigines.

The most plausible answer to megafaunal extinction is that different processes were at work on different continents. Direct or indirect human impact may have played an important role where unusually high levels of extinction occurred.

OUR PRIMATE ANCESTORS

Although the primates are a very small group of placental mammals, we humans have a vested interest in the history of our relatives. In 1735 the Swedish botanist Carl Linnaeus attempted the first systematic classification of all life as was known at that time. By 1758 it had gone through ten editions and accumulated the names of nearly 12,000 species of plants and animals compared with today's estimates of between 5 and 20 million species. It was in the tenth edition of his *Systema Naturae* that Linnaeus first placed humans in the order Anthropomorpha alongside the apes and monkeys. Although criticized for associating humans with such creatures, he challenged anyone to find significant anatomical differences that would warrant a different classification. Linnaeus subsequently changed the name to the order Primates and his classification is still used today. Now the order is known to include humans, apes, gibbons, monkeys, tarsiers, lorises, galagos, lemurs and their fossil ancestors.

Primates are and were typically small to medium-sized and omnivorous tree-dwellers, ranging in weight from the 30g pygmy mouse lemur to the 180kg gorilla. With bodies adapted for four-limbed climbing agility, they have acute eyesight and distance judgement, brain development and exhibit parental care. Anatomical changes from their insectivore ancestors include opposable thumbs and toes and flat nails instead of claws. In the skull the snout is reduced and the large closely spaced eyes point forwards to give stereoscopic vision and good distance judgement, and the brain is relatively large compared with body size. Only one or two babies are produced at a time, with prolonged pregnancy and maternal care leading to delayed sexual maturity and relatively long lives.

There are only around 69 genera and 376 species of primate living today and their fossil record is very patchy because their typically woodland and forest habitats are not particularly well preserved in the Cenozoic rock record. Most fossil remains are the teeth and the most indigestible bone fragments that have been left by predators and scavengers.

Modern biological and molecular-based classification makes a fundamental division between the strepsirhines (lemurs and lorises) and the haplorhines (tarsiers and anthropoids). The separation of the two groups dates back to the Eocene Epoch of the Early Cenozoic some 50 million years ago. Eocene times saw the appearance of both lemur-like adapid primates (such as *Cantius*, which weighed up to 7kg, from North America and Europe) and tiny tarsier-like tree-dwelling primates called omomyids (such as *Omomys* and *Shoshonius* from

North America). The latter were active; others were fruit-eaters.

Interestingly, they appeared along with perissodactyls and artiodactyls during a short-term interval of intense global warming when they dispersed across the northern continents.

Anthropoids

The anthropoids include the monkeys, gibbons, apes, humans and their fossil ancestors. The recent Chinese discovery of *Eosimias*, a primitive anthropoid in 45-million-year-old Middle Eocene strata, shows a combination of omomyid and New World monkey characters and may indicate an Asian rather than an African origin for the anthropoids.

Hominoids

The hominoids include the gibbons, apes and humans. Their origins are still problematic because of the poor fossil record of Oligocene apes. The best known, such as *Proconsul* from Africa, do not appear until Miocene times. By Late Miocene times, around 10 million years ago, the early apes had dispersed across Africa, Asia and into Europe. This epoch was the real 'planet of the apes', when they were most diverse and abundant. Tailless chimp-sized apes such as *Dryopithecus*, *Sivapithecus* and the recently discovered *Pierolapithecus* from Spain had short

Reconstruction of *Aegyptopithecus*, an Oligocene primate

snouts, forward-facing eyes and highly domed skulls. They were mostly tree-dwelling fruit-eaters and spread from the tropical forests of Africa into the woodlands of Europe and Asia.

Hominids

The hominids include the higher apes, humans and their fossil ancestors. Molecular analysis and comparison of the chimp and human DNA shows only a 1 per cent difference. According to the molecular clock, the divergence between the higher ape and human lineages occurred somewhere between 5 and 8 million years ago. Darwin realized that since our nearest living relatives the chimps are restricted to

Africa, it was most likely that we share a common African ancestor with them.

Human-related fossils, like those of other anthropoids, are rare and those that do occur are mostly very fragmentary, consisting of teeth and fragments of jaw and skull bones along with other physically tough parts of the skeleton. Post-mortem preservation of human-related remains requires rapid burial in sediment to prevent scavenging and further biological, physical and chemical degradation. The sediment then has to be protected from reworking by more regional subsidence.

Only certain geological environments tend to produce such a chain of events and the Great East African Rift Valley is one of them. The Rift Valley has the added benefit of frequent volcanism with the eruption of ash clouds and lavas that blanket the surrounding landscapes and help protect sediments and their fossils. In addition the volcanic lavas and ash deposits can be used to radiometrically date adjacent fossils. Many of the human-related fossils in Africa have been found in the Rift Valley. The other main source has been limestone cave sediments, especially in southern Africa, Europe and Asia.

Today over 20 human-related species are known to have lived over the last 7 million years or so, of which only one survives today – our species, *Homo sapiens*. The oldest of these hominid fossils is the 7-million-year-old *Sahelanthropus tchadensis* from central Africa (and one of the few found outside the Rift Valley). Its well preserved skull shows that this was a very apelike, metre-high animal with a chimp-sized brain and a mixture of primitive and more advanced features. It has been claimed that this animal could walk upright, but this is not proven.

Two other genera of similar creatures (*Orrorin* and *Ardipithecus*) are known from African strata 6–5 million years old. Again there are indications that they were upright walking, although their brains were still small and apelike. Global climates were changing as the Earth slid inexorably towards a series of ice ages. The effect in Africa was increasing dryness and the break up of the forests with the development of savannah, grasslands and patchy woodlands. Bipedalism would certainly have been advantageous for these small apelike creatures in travelling from one cluster of food plants to another. Bipedalism freed up the hands for carrying food and offspring and perhaps defensive weapons in the form of sticks and stones.

By around 4 million years ago there was a significant expansion in the hominids with the evolution of some ten species of australopithecines, such as the famous *Australopithecus afarensis*, nicknamed 'Lucy' by its discoverer, American anthropologist Don Johanson in 1974. We can be certain these were upright-walking creatures because of the remarkable 1978 discovery by Mary Leakey's team of 3.5-million-year-old footprints at Laetoli in Tanzania. The australopithecines were still small in stature and brain size, but there was a divergence into 'robust' and 'gracile' species. The former had specialized jaws and teeth for eating tough plant material such as nuts and roots, whilst the latter have more advanced smaller teeth and may well have been more omnivorous and perhaps scavengers that included some meat in their diet.

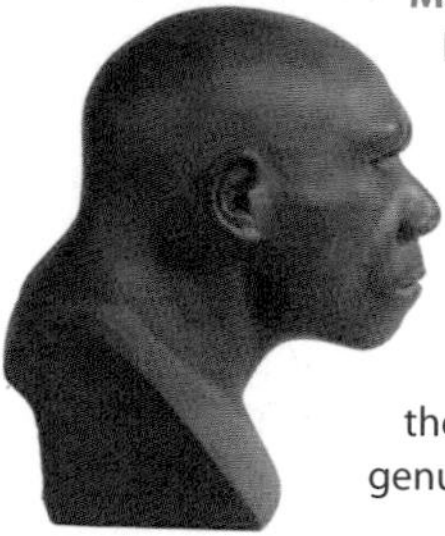

Membership of the genus *Homo*

Early membership of the genus *Homo* is still argued about, especially with regard to Louis Leakey's species *H. habilis* and whether it should be placed in *Australopithecus* or *Homo* depending upon what is taken as the threshold brain size for our genus. Brain size had risen from an apelike volume of around 400cc to 470cc in the australopithecines and just under 700cc in *H. habilis*, but some experts argue that the threshold should be higher at 750cc or more. However, there is archaeological evidence that the

Reconstruction of a male Neanderthal (*Homo neanderthalensis*)

manufacture of primitive stone tools had been innovated by 2.6 million years ago. Although Louis Leakey was convinced that his 'handyman' *H. habilis* was first to do this, it is not proven.

By the beginning of the Pleistocene, around 1.8 million years ago, global climates were changing rapidly and there was increasing aridity in Africa. Fossils of a new species known as *H. ergaster* in Africa, which is very similar to a Eurasian species *H. erectus*, show that for the first time close human relatives became widespread. They were upright-walking individuals, some of which may have grown to 1.8m with brain sizes of 800–900cc. They made stone tools and were by now effective meat-eating hunters although they probably also ate a variety of plant matter when available. It is generally argued that they spread from Africa north to Eurasia and northeast to Asia by 1.8 million years ago. With lowered sea levels during a cold glacial event in high latitudes, they were able to reach the island of Java.

A dwarf human-related species?

One of the most recent and intriguing human-related finds has been that of a dwarfed human species within cave deposits on the Indonesian island of Flores. *Homo floresiensis*, nicknamed 'the hobbit', grew to no more than a metre high with a brain size of 380cc, and yet is claimed to have been a member of our genus, thus breaking any previous brain-sized definition of *Homo*, even when the small body size is taken into account. A well-preserved skull and other bones have been dated at around 18,000 years old, which displaces the Neanderthals as the last survivors of our extinct relatives. They are claimed to show anatomical connections with and descent from *Homo erectus* who first occupied the region 1.6 million years ago.

The *H. floresiensis* fossils were found with stone tools and fossils of the dwarf elephant *Stegodon* and a giant monitor lizard. It cannot be proven that 'the hobbit' people made the tools, which have an age range of between 38,000 and 18,000 years old, but there are no other human-related remains associated with them.

Molecular DNA analysis of modern human populations shows a remarkable degree of genetic similarity despite superficial differences between populations in terms of average heights, body build, pigmentation and so on. The implication is that the dispersal of anatomically modern humans of our species *H. sapiens* has a remarkably recent origin, probably within the last 120,000 years and from Africa, where the remains of early members of the species have recently been found and named as the subspecies *H. s. idaltu*. Altogether, within our genus there are at least six species that have lived over the last 2.6 million years.

The Neanderthals

Most famous of all the extinct species is perhaps *Homo neanderthalensis*, known as the Neanderthal people. They were a Eurasian species of successful hunters who lived between 350,000 and 28,000 years ago. Their brains were as big as ours (1,100–1,400cc) but organized in a slightly different way, so that although they probably had speech it may not have been complex – syntactical language. It was thought that the Neanderthals were the ancestors of modern Eurasians, but anatomical and recent DNA analysis shows that this is highly unlikely. Nevertheless, we probably share a common ancestor with the Neanderthals. So who were our immediate ancestors?

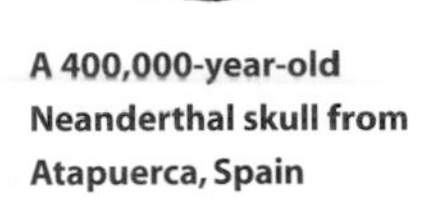

A 400,000-year-old Neanderthal skull from Atapuerca, Spain

Homo heidelbergensis

The most likely candidate is *Homo heidelbergensis*, whose remains were found in Germany in 1907 and dated to around 500,000 years old. Since then, fossils of this species have been found in southern England, through northern Spain to Africa where they were first named as a separate species

H. rhodesiensis. They have skulls with prominent bony brow-ridges and low foreheads but relatively large brains (1,200–1,300cc) like the Neanderthals but with longer and more slender limb bones. They evolved from a *H. ergaster/erectus* ancestor in Africa and subsequently gave rise to early members of *H. sapiens* in Africa, perhaps as long ago as 300,000 years.

Homo sapiens

From the African *H. sapiens*, the first move of modern humans occurred around 120,000–100,000 years ago northwards into the Middle East, where their fossils have been dated at around 100,000 years old. Modern humans reached Australia by around 50,000 years ago, Europe by around 35,000 years ago and the Americas perhaps before 20,000 years ago. However, the timing of arrival in North America is a highly contentious issue with some experts arguing that it did not happen until 15,000 years ago or less. The last regions to be occupied were the Pacific islands and New Zealand, which was not reached until AD1000.

Our global expansion over 100,000 years or so from a few tens of thousand to nearly 6 billion is remarkable. It can only have been achieved through significant levels of group cooperation and communication plus adaptability to local environments and circumstances. Finally, there was the considerable drive needed to overcome enormous physical and climatic barriers.

COLLECTING FOSSIL 'SHELLS'

The most common fossils are those of sea-dwelling shellfish, but in places the record of some life on land is well preserved. By recognizing what particular sediments represent in terms of their original depositional environments, the collector can target those situations that would have been favourable to particular groups of fossils.

Much of the popularity of fossils stems from the fact that many of them can easily be found and collected by the enthusiast. Even our Neanderthal relatives seem to have been intrigued by fossils. Hand axes have been found, tens of thousands of years old, which have been carefully made around fossil shells that naturally occur in Cretaceous flints found in Europe. In Palaeolithic times, modern humans made personal ornaments from fossils shells and bits of amber, and ever since fossils have been objects of human curiosity.

The nature and form of fossils has stimulated many myths over the millennia from providing evidence for the existence of giants, dragons, the Noachian Flood to works of the devil. Since the 17th century it has become increasingly evident that fossils are the remains of once living organisms.

Over the last few hundred years both amateur and professional collectors have made major contributions to our understanding of different fossil

Fossil trilobites in uplifted ancient seabeds in the Rocky Mountains, North America

groups. By devoting much time and effort to their hobby, amateurs have found and recovered many fossils that would otherwise have been lost to science. Many amateurs have gone on to make significant contributions to the scientific study of fossils.

FOSSIL OCCURRENCE

Sedimentary rock strata containing abundant fossils occur all over the world. Fossiliferous strata are commonly found exposed along rocky coastlines and in hilly terrain, although such locations also expose many other rock types that are not fossiliferous. For instance, rocks that have formed from a molten state (so-called igneous rocks such as granite and basalt) and rocks that have been heated and deformed by powerful earth movements (known as metamophic rocks, for example schist and gneiss) do not normally contain fossils.

Anyone starting out to collect fossils for the first time is best advised to visit the nearest museum with a collection of fossils or contact the nearest fossil collectors' association to get advice on where to start looking within your particular area. For instance, in the USA a permit is required for collecting vertebrate fossils. Amateurs are strongly encouraged to join organized museum trips where they can work in safety alongside professionals who have the necessary permits. As some recent cases have demonstrated, there are stiff penalties for unauthorized collecting on public lands.

There are some rules about responsible collecting. Safe procedures must be followed, private land must be respected – do not climb, dig or cross private property without the permission of the property owner. Take care to look after your finds properly.

Safety procedures

Before you set out, you should be properly equipped and should tell someone where you are going and when you will return. Carry a mobile phone if you have one. Wear a hard hat at any rock outcrop: an apple-sized pebble falling 20m onto your head can kill you unless you are wearing a proper safety helmet. Safety goggles must be worn when hammering rocks, flying splinters can blind you. Rock hammers and chisels rather than carpenter's hammers must be used. Maps and compasses should be carried and protective clothing should be worn if you are hiking off the beaten track. Bring an ample supply of drinking water.

Any rock outcrop is potentially hazardous, especially cliffs or quarry faces that can collapse without warning. Removing rocks from the base of such an outcrop inevitably makes the rocks less stable and prone to fall. Do not forget to check out the locality to make sure it is not a protected site or private land before you even start looking or collecting fossils.

Once at your selected site, the first thing to do is to check for any other potential hazards such as incoming tides, flash floods and the like, and make sure you know your exit route. Note where you are on your map or in a notebook with sufficient care that you can be sure to be able to return to exactly the same spot. Many a frustrating hour has been lost trying to relocate a particularly good find.

The best way to find fossils is firstly to search over any loose rock lying about. You can survey a much greater surface area this way than by trying to break open rocks. It will also give you an idea of the different kinds of rock to be found and which are the most fossiliferous. Only when you have exhausted these possibilities should you turn to fresh rocks.

The techniques of safely and effectively breaking open rocks needs to be learned and it is sensible to start off collecting with someone who is experienced.

Although many rock strata are very hard, the fossils they contain are often surprisingly delicate or fragile. Good fossils can easily be ruined by careless handling. Labels, a field notebook and waterproof pens and pencils will finish off your gear. Specimens need to be carefully labelled with their exact location (again a GPS unit is invaluable here). They then have to be wrapped in protective paper and sometimes in softer material, such as cotton or synthetic wadding, to protect them.

When you unwrap your specimens make sure you transfer the locality details to the specimen, ideally with a small unobtrusive label glued to the rock surface. The specimen should be protected by a box in which further locality details and other information, especially its scientific name, can be placed when you know it.

If you think that you have found an interesting fossil, show it to an expert at your local museum or college – it may be of scientific importance.

HOW TO IDENTIFY FOSSILS

Most fossils only preserve hard parts such as shells and skeletons and tough plant materials such as woody tissues. Consequently, identification of the remains is dependent upon physical characters preserved by those hard parts and any indirect evidence for soft-part anatomy. Fossil species are therefore different from biological species. Fortunately, many fossil groups ranging from single-celled protists such as the foraminifers to clam shells and mammal teeth show a close correspondence between fossil and biological species.

In the past, variations in the mineralogical composition of fossils confused scientists as to their real identity as once-living organisms. But now we have a much better understanding of how shells and bones can be replaced by minerals such as iron pyrites and how woody tissues can be replaced by opal and agate. Indeed, mineralization can preserve anatomical details, such as cell shape and structure, that are vital to accurate identification of species, detail that would otherwise be lost during fossilization.

Fossil form is so variable that it is difficult to produce a simple key to identification as can be done for plants. However, many fossils preserve enough characteristic features that allow their assignation to well known taxonomic groups even down to the ordinal level. For instance, it is not too difficult for the experienced amateur to readily recognize plant groups, such as clubmosses (lycopsids), mammal teeth or molluscan shells belonging to major groups of clams and snails.

But there are quite a lot of fossils that are not so easy for the non-expert to categorize. For example, bivalved fossil shells may belong to molluscan clams, which are still common today, or to the unrelated lampshells (brachiopods). The latter are rare today but were common in the Palaeozoic. With practice, it soon becomes possible to recognize their distinguishing features.

In general, most visible plant fossils are leaves, bits of plant stem and some resilient reproductive structures such as seeds. These are commonly preserved as black or dark-coloured carbonized remains of the original leaf material. The major groups of plants tend to have reasonably distinctive features, such as leaf shapes and venation patterns, but in detail they can be much more difficult to tell apart. For instance, many extinct seed-plants (gymnosperms) had leaf fronds that superficially look like those of ferns (filicaleans).

Of the relatively simple invertebrate groups with preservable remains, foraminifers, bryozoans, sponges and corals are the most important. The single-celled foraminifers are incredibly abundant in some marine sediments, although their coiled shells are mostly microscopic and difficult for the non-expert to identify. By comparison, sponges can generally be recognized by their overall form, the shape and composition of their spicules (made up of silica and calcium carbonate) and porous walls; corals build a supporting structures of calcium carbonate with distinctive patterns of internal plates.

The shelled invertebrates that form the bulk of the fossil record belong to a few major groups, especially the molluscs (clams, snails and various cephalopods), lampshells (brachiopods), arthropods (especially the trilobites, eurypterids and various crustaceans) and echinoderms (sea-urchins, starfish and sea-lilies). Most of them build shells or skeletons either wholly or partly of calcium carbonate.

Clams can be distinguished by their two-hinged valves, which also have discernible growth lines and various patterns of ribs and spines. These patterns are also seen on the typically coiled shells of the snails, many of which grow in a helical spiral. Many of the cephalopods such as the nautiloids, ammonoids, goniatites and ammonites also have coiled shells, but they are mostly planispiral and chambered. The extinct squid-like belemnites had a bullet-shaped internal skeleton, but most of the other soft-bodied molluscs, such as the octopus, squid and sea-hares, have little in the way of a fossil record.

Lampshells (brachiopods), similar to clams, have two valves connected by a hinge and muscles, but also have important differences that can be distinguished with practice. For instance, one valve is generally bigger than the other and the bigger valve's curved beak has a hole at its apex. Brachiopods varied considerably in shape throughout their long evolutionary history and many can be readily identified at the family and genus level.

Arthropods are characterized by their exoskeletons and jointed appendages. Major fossil groups such as the trilobites can be relatively easily distinguished by their body form, but individual species can be much more difficult to tell apart. Much of the fossil record of arthropods depends on the mineralization of the exoskeleton. Groups such as the trilobites and crustaceans are well represented but other such as the insects and eurypterids less so. Growth by repeated moulting in many arthropods also increases their fossil record.

Echinoderms are marine animals forming distinctive groups such as the starfish, sea-urchins and sea-lilies, with an ancient fossil record. Fossil echinoderms are relatively common because of the mineralization of their skeletons with calcium carbonate. Many of them have multi-element skeletons, which greatly increases the chances of some parts being preserved. Most can be easily recognized at the genus or family level when the skeleton is well preserved, but individual bits are rarely so identifiable. A common feature is the five-fold symmetry shown by most groups of echinoderms.

The graptolites are an extinct group of marine colonial organisms that are close to primitive chordates and have an important fossil record. Their organic-walled skeletons are common in some Lower Palaeozoic sedimentary strata and are typically preserved as serrated fronds with characteristic branching patterns. Rapid evolution and distinctive form means that they can be used for relative dating of their host strata.

Conodonts are very small toothed structures of variable shape made of calcium phosphate, which are common in some Palaeozoic limestones. The conodont elements form the hard tissue part of a feeding apparatus for the extinct conodont animals. Experts have distinguished many species that are of considerable use in the relative dating of strata.

The backboned (vertebrate) animals are now known to have a long history extending back into Late Cambrian times with an even earlier Cambrian ancestry. There are a number of familiar groups with distinctive form, such as the fish, amphibians, reptiles, birds and mammals. However, there are also a number of less familiar extinct groups, some of which fit easily into these groupings and some that do not, such as some agnathan 'fish' and early tetrapods.

All vertebrates are characterized by an internal vertebral skeleton and most have associated structures such as a skull, girdles and appendages. Most of these skeletal elements are mineralized with calcium phosphate except for a major group of fish that includes the sharks and is cartilaginous. Some vertebrates, such as certain extinct agnathans, fish, dinosaurs and mammals, also had bony elements that made up a dermal protective armour.

Major groups of vertebrates can be distinguished by their fossil skeletal remains and many can be specifically identified by experts on the basis of a few bones or even a single tooth, but many others require more complete fossils.

Trace fossils

The identity of many trace fossils can be peculiarly difficult beyond a general level of recognition such as sauropod dinosaur footprint, u-shaped worm burrow and so on. However, experts can often assign individual traces to 'ichnogenera' and 'species', but only a small portion of these can be matched with the fossil organism that made them.

SOURCES OF INFORMATION

Websites

www.ucmp.berkeley.edu
www.nhm.ac.uk
www.nmnh.si.edu/paleo
www.PaleoBase.com

Books

Benton, M. (2005) *Vertebrate Palaeontology*, 3rd edn. Blackwell Science, Oxford.

Brasier, M.D. (2004) *Microfossils*. Blackwell Science, Oxford.

Briggs, D.E.G. and Crowther, P.R. (2001) *Palaeobiology* II. Blackwell Science, Oxford.

Clarkson, E.N.K. (1998) *Invertebrate Palaeontology and Evolution*. Blackwell Science, Oxford.

Erwin, Douglas H. (2006) *Extinction*. Princeton UP, Princeton.

Feduccia, A. (1999) *Origin and Evolution of Birds*, 2nd edn. Yale UP, New Haven.

Kenrick, P. and Davis, P. (2004) *Fossil Plants*. Natural History Museum, London.

Palmer, D. (2000) *Atlas of the Prehistoric World* (rev. edn). Marshall Publishing, London.

Palmer, D. (2003) *Fossil Revolution: The Finds that Changed our View of the Past*. HarperCollins, London.

Palmer, D. (2003) *Prehistoric Past Revealed: The Four Billion Year History of Life on Earth*. Mitchell Beazley, London.

Prothero, D.R. (1998) *Bringing Fossils to Life: an Introduction to Paleobiology*. W.C.B./McGraw-Hill, New York.

Stringer, C. and Andrews, P. (2005) *The Complete World of Human Evolution*. Thames and Hudson London, England.

GLOSSARY

Australopithecines 'Southern apes', a large group of 1m tall, small-brained but upright-walking apes that lived in Africa from 4.2–1.3 million years ago.
Biostratigraphy The study of the subdivision of strata according to their fossil content.
Biozone A sequence of strata defined by a particular assemblage of fossils.
Cartilage A tough but flexible and non-mineralized tissue forming the basis of the vertebrate skeleton; generally replaced by bone except in the cartilaginous (chondrichthyan) fishes.
Chloroplasts Chlorophyll-containing organelles that occur in plant and algal cells undergoing photosynthesis.
Coelenterates A large group of invertebrates, including jellyfish and corals, whose body walls are made of two cell layers surrounding a body cavity with one opening to the exterior.
Co-evolution The contemporary appearance of complementary adaptations in two species that arise through the selection pressures that they impose on one another.
Colony A group of individuals who live together, are dependent upon one another, and have a close genetic relationship.
Convergent evolution The appearance of similar structures in unrelated organisms, generally as adaptations to similar environmental selection pressures, for example the wings of insects, bats and birds.
Cyanobacteria A large group of eubacteria that obtain food energy through similar processes of photosynthesis used by green plants and algae.

Cyst The enclosing membrane of a resting structure in the life history of certain organisms, especially microscopic ones, often strengthened and protected against the elements.
Dermal Pertaining to the skin or dermis.
DNA Deoxyribonucleic acid, the genetic material that controls protein synthesis and determines heredity.
Eubacteria A group of prokaryotes that comprise the majority of bacteria, including both aerobic and anaerobic species.
Food chain A linked sequence of organisms whose consumption of one another results in the transfer of energy, for example, carnivores eat herbivores; herbivores eat plants.
Girdles Skeletal structures that support the limbs and link them to the backbone in vertebrates, that is, the pelvic and pectoral girdles for the legs and arms respectively.
Lignin A complex organic polymer that secondarily thickens the cellulose walls of plant cells to make woody tissue.
Megafauna All those animals whose body mass is greater than 40kg.
Metamorphosis A major transformational event in the life history of an organism, especially from the larval to adult stage, that involves significant reorganization.
Molecular clock The theoretical device for the timing of evolutionary divergence based on the claim that average molecular substitution rates are constant and can be compared with the genetic distance between living organisms to calculate their original date of divergence from a common ancestor.
Ooze A very fine-grained muddy deposit that may be made of organic remains, such as coccoliths, or inorganic material, such as volcanic dust.
Permafrost Permanently frozen ground in polar regions.

Photosynthesis The chemical process by which organic compounds (carbohydrates) are built up from carbon dioxide and water in the presence of sunlight.
Placenta The organ that attaches an embryo to the wall of the uterus, connecting the embryo to the maternal blood system and providing it with nourishment.
Pollination The transfer of plant pollen from the male reproductive organ (the anther) to the female organ (the stigma) prior to fertilization, often involving an agent, such as an animal or inanimate process.
Segment One of a number of repeated divisions of an animal body that arise during embryonic development and contain similar organs.
Speciation The evolutionary process whereby one or more new species are derived from an ancestral one when interbreeding can no longer occur between populations.
Stigma The sticky surface on a plant's female reproductive organ to which pollen is attached during pollination.
Supercontinent An amalgamation of tectonic plates through the processes of ocean floor spreading and subduction.
Tectonic Those earth processes whereby rocks are moved and transformed from one state into another.
Tectonic plate A large rigid section of the rocky surface layers of the Earth.
Tetrapod A backboned animal (vertebrate) with four limbs.
Tubercle A prominent structure arising from the surface of a tissue and to which other structures may be attached.
Understorey A lower level of plant growth beneath the main uppermost tree canopy.
Zooid An individual member of an invertebrate animal colony. It is often produced by asexual reproduction.

INDEX

Note: page numbers in **bold** refer to captions.